THE RENT VEIL

BY HORATIUS BONAR

CONTENTS

PREFACE

The Epistle to the Hebrews was written by the eternal Spirit for the whole Church of God in all ages. It shows us on what footing we are to stand before God as sinners; and in what way we are to draw near as worshippers.

It assumes throughout, that the present condition of the Church on earth is one continually requiring the application of the great sacrifice for cleansing. The theory of personal sinlessness has no place in it. Continual evil, failure, imperfection, are assumed as the condition of God's worshippers on earth, during this dispensation. Personal imperfection on the one hand, and vicarious perfection on the other, are the solemn truths which pervade the whole. There is no day nor hour in which evil is not coming forth from us, and in which the great bloodshedding is not needed to wash it away. This epistle is manifestly meant for the whole life of the saint, and for the whole history of the Church. God's purpose is that we should never, while here, get beyond the need of expiation and purging; and though vain man may think that he would better glorify God by sinlessness, yet the Holy Spirit in this epistle shows us that we are called to glorify God by our perpetual need of the precious bloodshedding upon the cross. No need of washing, may be the watchword of some; they are beyond all that! But they who, whether conscious or unconscious of sin, will take this epistle as the declaration of God's mind as to the imperfection of the believing man on earth, will be constrained to acknowledge that the bloodshedding must be in constant requisition, not (as some say) to keep the believer in a sinless state, but to cleanse him from his hourly sinfulness.[1]

Boldness to enter into the holiest is a condition of the soul which can only be maintained by continual recourse to the blood of sprinkling, alike for conscious and for unconscious sin: the latter of these being by far the most subtle and the most terrible,--that for which the sin-offering required to be brought.

"If we say that we have no sin, we deceive ourselves, and the truth is not in us." The presence of sin in us is the only thing which makes such epistles as that to the Hebrews at all intelligible. When, by some instantaneous act of faith, we soar above sin, (as some think they do) we also bid farewell to the no longer needed blood, and to the no longer needed Epistle to the Hebrews.

"Through the veil, which is His flesh," is our one access to God; not merely at first when we believed, but day by day, to the last. The blood- dropped pavement is that one which we tread, and the blood-stained mercy-seat is that before which we bow. In letters of blood there is written on that veil, and that mercy-seat, "I am the way, the truth, and the life; no man cometh to the Father but by me": and, again, "Through Him we have access, by one Spirit, unto the Father."

Every thing connected with the sanctuary, outer and inner, is, in God's sight, excellent and precious. As of the altar, so of every other part of it, we may say, "Whatsoever toucheth it shall be holy" (Exo 29:37). Or, as the Apostle Peter puts it, "To you who believe this preciousness belongs" (1 Peter 2:7, i.e., all the preciousness of the "precious stone").

Men may ask, May we not be allowed to differ in opinion from God about this preciousness? Why should our estimate of the altar, or the blood, or the veil, if not according to God's, be so fatal to us as to shut us out of the kingdom? And why should our acceptance of God's estimate make us heirs of salvation? I answer, such is the mind of God, and such is the divine statute concerning admission and exclusion.

You may try the experiment of differing from Him as to other things, but beware of differing from Him as to this. Remember that He has said, "This is my beloved Son, in whom I am well pleased." Say what you like, He is a jealous God, and will avenge all disparagement of His sanctuary, or dishonour of His Son. Contend with Him, if you will try the strife, about other things. It may not cost you your soul. Dispute His estimate of the works of His hand in heaven and earth; say that they are not altogether "good," and that you could have improved them, had you been consulted. It may not forfeit your crown. Tell Him that His light is not so glorious as He thinks it is, nor His stars so brilliant as He declares they are. He may bear with this thy underrating of His material handiwork, and treat thee as a foolish child that speaks of what he knows not.

But touch His great work, His work of works,-- the person and propitiation of His only-begotten Son, and He will bear with thee no more. Differ from Him in His estimate of the great bloodshedding, and he will withstand thee to the face. Tell Him that the blood of Golgotha could no more expiate sin than the blood of bulls and of goats, and He will resent it to the uttermost. Depreciate anything, everything that He has made; He may smile at thy presumption. But depreciate not the cross. Underrate not the sacrifice of the great altar. It will cost thee thy soul. It will shut thee out of the kingdom. It will darken thy eternity.

The Grange, Edinburgh, October 1874

[1] I intended to have said something more upon this point; but room fails me. I meant to have noticed the Seventh of the Romans in connection with some recent opinions. But I content myself with the following letter, which appeared in the London Record of October 19th, to show the extreme lengths to which some are prepared to go in advocating their tenets. Rather than reconsider their own opinions, they will affirm that the Apostle Paul fell from grace, went into heresy, and that the Seventh of the Romans is the confession of his fall and heresy. An English Clergyman thus writes to the London Record:-- "I am surprised that in dealing with Mr. Pearsall Smith's errors, no one, so far as I know, has yet called attention to his tract, 'Bondage and Liberty,' on the Seventh of Romans. "He asserts that St. Paul 'fell from grace,' and became entangled in the Galatian heresy! That there may be no kind of mistake, I give his own words:-- "'But having begun in the Spirit, he had sought to be made perfect by the activities of the flesh, the consequences of which were that sin revived and "he died," or lost his full communion with Christ, and victory through faith over sin. "'You have had now to travel along with Paul in the Seventh of Romans, in this passage which is manifestly the experience of a Christian, though not a true Christian experience. After having once exclaimed, "How shall we that are dead to sin live any longer therein?" you have been deceived, mistaking your own efforts to keep God's law for the walk of faith; and the result has been that sin has been--not conquered, but to a sad extent manifested. "'It is this agonising experience of yours of failure in your inward and outward walk that was shared by Paul in this parenthesis--following his declaration of the death of believers to sin and to the law--to which he here limits the pronoun "I," as the acknowledgment of how a Christian may fail, rather than as belonging to the proper experience of a Christian. It was this experience that made him so zealous in warning the Galatians against legalism in their walk. It was the agony of this "falling from grace" and coming "under law" in his practical ways that brought out the cry of despair, "O wretched man that I am! who shall deliver me from the body of this death?" "'But, brother Paul, thy agony is ended when, as in a moment, and with a sudden joy that precludes explana-

tion, thou again beholdest Jesus dawning on thy soul as a Deliverer, not only from wrath, but from sinning. "I thank God through Jesus Christ our Lord."' "As may be supposed, there is much nonsense and confusion in the little book from which the above is taken, but I submit whether there is not something worse, and which calls for vigorous treatment at the hands of faithful, sensible, Evangelical men?"

Chapter 1

Open Intercourse with God

It does not seem a strange thing that the creature and the Creator should meet face to face, and that they should hold intercourse without any obstructing medium.

We may not understand the mode of communication between the visible and the invisible, but we can see this, at least, that He who made us can communicate with us, by the ear or the eye or the touch. He can speak and we can hear; and, again, we can speak and He can hear. His being and ours can thus come together, to interchange thought and affection: He giving, we receiving; He rejoicing in us, and we rejoicing in Him: He loving us, and we loving Him. He can look on us, and we can look on Him; He "guiding us with His eye" (Psa 32:8), and we fixing our eye on His, as children on the eye of a father, taking in all the love and tenderness which beam from His paternal look, and sending up to Him our responding look of filial confidence and love. Not that He has "eyes of flesh, or seeth as man seeth" (Job 10:4); but He can fix His gaze on us in ways of His own, and make us feel His gaze, as really as when the eyes of friends look into each other's depths. "He that formed the eye shall He not see" (Psa 94:9). He who made the human eye to be "the light of the body" (Matt 6:22),--that organ through which light enters the body,-- in order that He might pour into us the glory of His own sun and moon and stars,--can He not, through some inner eye which we know not, and for which we have no name, pour into us the radiance of His own infinite glory, though He be the "King invisible" (1 Tim 1:17),--He "whom no man hath seen nor can see" (1 Tim 6:16),--the "invisible God" (Col 1:15). He can touch us; for in Him we live and move and have our being:[2] and we can lay hold of Him, for He is not far from any one of us; He is the nearest of all that is near, and the most palpable of all the palpable. It would seem, then, that open and free and near intercourse with the God who made us arose from His being what He is, and from our being what we are: as if it were a necessity both of His existence and of ours.

That He should be our Creator, and yet be separated from us, seems an impossibility; that we should be His creatures, and yet remain at a distance from Him, seems the most unnatural and unlikely of all relations. Intercourse, fellowship, mutual love, then, seem to flow from all that He is to us, and from all that we are to Him.

We can conceive of no obstruction, no difficulty in all this, so long as we remained what He has made us. There could be nothing but the sympathy of heart with heart; a flow and reflow of holy and unobstructed love.

Unhindered access to the God who made us seems one of the necessary conditions of our nature; and this not arising out of any merit or worthiness on the part of the creature, but from the fitness of things; the adaptation of the thing made to Him who made it; and the impossibility of separation between that which was made and Him who made it. The life above and the life below must draw together; heart cannot be separated from heart, unless something come between to put asunder that which had by the necessity of nature been joined together. Distance from God does not belong to our creation, but has come in as something unnatural, something alien to creative love, something which contravenes the original and fundamental law of our being.

The tree separated from its root, the flower broken off from its stem, are the fittest emblems of man disjoined from God. Such distance seems altogether unnatural. The want of vital connection, in our original constitution, or the absence of sympathy, would imply defect in the workmanship, of the most serious kind,--and no less would it indicate imperfection on the part of the Great Worker.

God made us for Himself; that He might delight in us and we in Him; He to be our portion and we His; He to be our treasure and we His.[3] He made us after His own likeness; so that each part of our being has its resemblance or counterpart in Himself: our affections, and sympathies, and feelings being made after the model of His own. We are apt to associate God only with what is cold and abstract and ideal; ourselves with what is emotional and personal. Herein we greatly err. We must reverse the picture if we would know the truth concerning Him with whom is no coldness, no abstraction, no impersonality. The reality pertaining to the nature of man, is as nothing when compared with the reality belonging to the nature of Him who created us after His own image. In so far as the infinite exceeds the finite, in so far does that which we call reality transcend in God all that is known by that term in man. We are the shadows, He is the substance. Jehovah is the infinitely real and true and personal: and it is with Him as such that we have to do. The God of philosophy may be a cold abstraction, which no mind can grasp, and by which no heart can be warmed; but the God of Scripture, the God who created the heavens and the earth, the God and Father of our Lord Jesus Christ, is a reality,--a reality for both the mind and heart of man. It is the infinite Jehovah that loves, and pities, and blesses; who bids us draw near to Him, walk with Him, and have fellowship with Him. It is the infinite Jehovah who fills the finite heart; for He made that heart for the very purpose of its being filled with Himself. Our joy is to be in Him; His joy is in us. Over us He resteth in His love, and in Himself He bids us rest. Apart from Him creaturehood has neither stability nor blessedness.

Free and open intercourse with the God who made us, is one of the necessities of our being. Acquaintanceship with Him, and delight in Him, are the very life of our created existence. Better not to be than not to know Him, in whom we live, and move, and have our being. Better to pass away into unconsciousness or nothingness, than to cease to delight in Him, or to be delighted in by Him.

The loss of God is the loss of everything; and in having God we have everything. His overflowing fulness is our inheritance; and in nearness to Him we enjoy that fulness. He cannot speak to us, but something of that fulness flows in. We cannot speak to Him without attracting His excellency towards us. This mutual speech, or converse, is that which forms the medium of communication between heaven and earth. Man looketh up, and God looketh down: our eyes meet, and we are, in the twinkling of an eye, made partakers of the divine abundance.[4] Man speaks out to God what He feels; God speaks out to man what He feels. The finite and the infinite mind thus interchange their sympathies; love meets love, mingling and rejoicing together; the full pours itself into the empty, and the empty receiveth the full.

The greatness of God is no hindrance to this intercourse: for one special part of the divine greatness is to be able to condescend to the littleness of created beings, seeing that creaturehood must, from its very nature, have this littleness; inasmuch as God must ever be God, and man must ever be man: the ocean must ever be the ocean, the drop must ever be the drop. The greatness of God compassing our littleness about, as the heavens the earth, and fitting into it on every side, as the air into all parts of the earth, is that which makes the intercourse so complete and blessed. "In His hand is the soul of every living thing, and the breath of all mankind" (Job 12:10). Such is His nearness to, such His intimacy with, the works of His hands.

It is nearness, not distance, that the name Creator implies; and the simple fact of His having made us is the assurance of His desire to bless us and to hold intercourse with us. Communication between the thing made and its maker is involved in the very idea of creation. "Thy hands have made me and fashioned me: give me understanding, that I may learn Thy commandments" (Psa 119:73). "Faithful Creator" is His name (1 Peter 4:19), and as such we appeal to Him, "Forsake not the work of Thine own hands" (Psa 138:8).

Nothing that is worthless or unloveable ever came from His hands; and as being His "workmanship," we may take the assurance of His interest in us, and His desire for converse with us.[5]

He put no barrier between Himself and us when He made us. If there be such a thing now, it is we who have been its cause. Separation from Him must have come upon our side. It was not the father who sent the younger son away; it was that son who "gathered all together and took his journey into the far country" (Luke 15:13), because he had become tired of the father's house and the father's company.

The rupture between God and man did not begin on the side of God. It was not heaven that withdrew from earth, but earth that withdrew from heaven. It was not the father that said to the younger son, Take your goods, pack up and be gone; it was that son who said, "Father give me the portion of goods that falleth to me," and who, "not many days after, took his journey into the far country," turning his back on his father and his father's house.

"O Israel! thou hast destroyed THYSELF" (Hosea 13:9). O man! thou hast cast off God. It is not God who has cast off thee. Thou hast dislinked thyself from the blessed Creator; thou hast broken the golden chain that fastened thee to His throne, the silken cord that bound thee to his heart.

Yet He wants thee back again; nor will He rest till He has accomplished His gracious design, and made thee once more the vessel of His love.

[2] 1. It is interesting to notice the way in which the negative particle is used in the different designations of God. He is called invisible,--He who cannot be seen, He who cannot lie (Titus 1:2) incorruptible (Rom 1:23; 1 Tim 1:17) He who cannot be tempted (James 1:13): He who only hath immortality (1 Tim 6:16). In connection with the things of God, and of Christ, we have a similar use of the same

negative particle:--Thus, "His eternal power and Godhead" (Rom 1:20); unfading (1 Peter 1:4); immutability (Heb 6:17); without repentance (Rom 11:29); undefiled (Heb 7:26); past finding out (Rom 11:33); unchangeable (Heb 7:24). These instances will illustrate the truth that very much of what we express of God, is expressed in the form of a contrast to the things of man.

[3] John Howe thus writes on this point, in his treatise on "Delighting in God":--"The most excellent portion, in whom all things that may render Him such do concur and meet together; all desirable and imaginable riches and fulness, together with large bounty, flowing goodness, every way correspondent to the wants and cravings of indigent and thirsty souls. How infinitely delightful is it to view and enjoy Him as our portion...every way complete and full, it being the all-comprehensive good which is this portion, God all-sufficient...making His boundless fulness overflow to the replenishing of thirsty longing souls."

[4] "How pleasant to lose themselves in Him; to be swallowed up in the overcoming sense of His boundless, all-sufficient, everywhere flowing fulness! By this dependence they make this fulness of God their own. They have nothing to do but to depend; to live upon a present self-sufficient good, which alone is enough to replenish all desires. How can we divide the highest pleasure, the fullest satisfaction, from this dependence! 'Tis to live at the rate of a god; a godlike life; a living upon immense fulness; as He lives."--Howe's Blessedness of the Righteous, Chapter 8.

[5] "God's excellency, His wisdom, His purity and love seemed to appear in everything; in the sun, moon, and stars; in the clouds and blue sky; in the grass, flowers, and trees; in the water, and all nature--which used greatly to fix my mind."--Jonathan Edwards

Chapter 2

How There Came to Be a Veil

There was no veil in Paradise between man and God. There were three places or regions; the outer earth, Eden, and "the Garden of Eden," or Paradise; but there was no veil nor fence between, hindering access from the one to the other. There was nothing to prevent man from going in to speak with God, or God from coming out to speak with man.

It was not till after man had disobeyed that the veil was let down which separated God from man, which made a distinction between the dwellings of man and the habitation of God.

Before God had spoken or done aught in the way of separation, man betrayed his consciousness of his new standing, and of the necessity for a covering or screen. He fled from God into the thick trees of the garden, that their foliage might hide him from God and God from him. In so doing he showed that he felt two things,-- 1. That there must be a veil between him and God; 2. That, now, in his altered position, distance from God (if such a thing could be) was his safety.

Even if God had said "draw near," man could not have responded "let us draw near," or felt "it is good for me to draw near to God." For sin had now come between, and until that should be dealt with in the way of pardon and removal, he could not approach God, nor expect God to approach him.

There was a sense of guilt upon his conscience, and he knew that there was displeasure on the part of God; so that fellowship, in such circumstances, was impossible. Any meeting, in this case, could only be that of the criminal and the Judge; the one to tremble, and the other to pronounce the righteous sentence.

God did come down to man; but not to converse as before; not to commune in love as if nothing had come in between them. He came to declare His righteousness; and yet to reveal His grace. He came to condemn, and He came to pardon. He came to show how utterly he abhorred the sin, and yet how graciously he was minded toward the sinner.

Something then had now come in between the Creator and the creature, which made it no longer possible for the same intercourse to be maintained as before. Man himself felt this, as soon as he had sinned; and God declared that it was so.

How was that "something" to be dealt with? It was of man's creation; yet man had no power to deal with it.

Shall it be removed, or shall it stand? If it stands, then man is lost to God and to himself. For the sentence is explicit, "In the day thou eatest thereof thou shalt surely die."[6] If it is to be removed, the barrier swept away, and the distance obliterated, God must do it, and He must do it immediately, before the criminal is handed over to final execution, and He must do it righteously, that there may be no uncertainty as to the thing done, and no possibility of any future reversal of the blessing or any replacement of the barrier.

God, in coming down to man, said, "Thou hast sinned, and there is not now the same relationship between us that there was: there is a barrier; but I mean to remove it; not all at once; and yet completely at last." Man was not to be lost to God, nor to himself. He was too precious a part of God's possessions to be thrown away. He was too dear to God to be destroyed. "God loved the world" (John 3:16).

Yet there must be a shutting out from God; and this was intimated from the beginning. God shuts Himself out from man; and He shuts man out from himself: for the way into the holiest for a sinner could not be prepared all at once. Not man only, but the universe, must be taught long lessons both in righteousness and in grace, before the new and living way can be opened.

Law had said "The soul that sinneth it shall die" (Eze 18:4); Grace had said "I have no pleasure in the death of the wicked" (Eze 33:11); Righteousness had said "The wicked shall be turned into hell" (Psa 9:17); Mercy had said "How shall I deliver thee up?" (Hosea 11:8). In what way are these things to be reconciled? Condemnation is just: can pardon be also just? Exclusion from God's presence was righteous, can admission into that presence be no less so?

The solution of this question must be given on judicial grounds, and must recognise all the judicial or legal elements involved in the treatment of crime and criminals. For law is law, and grace is grace. The two things cannot be intermingled. What law demands it must have; and what grace craves can only be given in accordance with unchanging law. "The reign of grace" must be "the reign of law"; and the triumph of grace must be the triumph of law. The grace which alone can reach the case of the sinner is the grace of the LAWGIVER, the grace of the JUDGE.

These were truths which man could not fully comprehend. They were new truths, or new ideas, which could only be thoroughly understood by long training, by ages of education. The method of instruction was peculiar, and such as suited man's special state of imperfect knowledge. It was twofold, consisting of a long line of revelations extending over four thousand years; and a long series of symbols increasing and becoming more expressive age after age.

That there was free love in God for the sinner was a new truth altogether, and needed to be fully revealed, "line upon line." Reasoning from God's treatment of the angels, man would conclude that there was no favour to be expected for the sinner; nothing but swift retribution, "everlasting chains." God's first words to man were those of grace; intimating that the divine treatment of man was to be very different from that of the fallen angels: that where sin had abounded grace was to abound much more. Forgiveness, not condemnation, was the essence of the early promise.

But this was only one-half of the great primal revelation. God having announced His purpose of grace, proceeds to show how this was to be carried out with full regard to the perfection of the law and the holiness of the Lawgiver.

The unfolding of this latter part of His purpose fills up the greater part of the Divine Word.

The announcement of God's free love was made on the spot where the sin had been committed and the transgressors arrested. But the unfolding of the plan, whereby that free love was to reach the sinner in righteousness, was commenced outside--at the gate of Paradise, where the first altar was built, the first sacrifice was offered, and the first sinner worshipped.

The blood-shedding was outside, and Paradise was closed against the sinner:--Paradise the type of that heavenly sanctuary from which man had shut himself out. No blood was shed within; for the place was counted holy; and besides, man, the sinner, was excluded from it now, and blood was only needed in connection with him and his entrance to God.

To shut out man the sword of fire was placed at the gate: teaching him not only that he was prohibited from entering, but that it was death to attempt an entrance. Paradise was not swept away; nay, man was allowed to build his altar and to worship at its gate; but he must remain outside in the meantime, till the great process had been completed, by which his nearer approach was secured,--not only without the dread of death, but with the assurance that there was life within for him.

But the flaming sword said, "Not now; not yet." Much must be done before man can be allowed to go in. "The Holy Ghost this signified that the way into the holiest was not yet made manifest."

In after ages there was no flaming sword at the gate. But the veil of the tabernacle was substituted instead of it. That veil said also, "Not now, not yet." Wait a little longer, O man, and the gate shall be thrown wide open. These sacrifices of yours have much to do in connection with the opening of the gate. Without them it cannot be opened; but even with them, a long time must elapse before this can be done; man must be taught that only righteousness can open that gate, and that this righteousness can only be unfolded and carried out by the blood-shedding of a substitute.

Man had been driven out in one hour; but he must wait ages before he can re-enter. In that interval of patient waiting he must learn many a lesson, both regarding God and himself; both regarding sin and righteousness; both regarding the reason of his being excluded and the way of re-admission.

For man is slow to learn. He cannot all at once take in new ideas as to God and His character. He must be fully "educated" in these; and this education must be one not of years but of ages.

God then began to teach man by means of sacrifice. This method of teaching him concerning grace and righteousness widened and filled up age after age. For this fuller education the tabernacle was set up; and there God commenced His school. By means of it He taught Israel, He taught man. The text- book was a symbolic one, though not without explanations and comments. It is contained in the Book of Leviticus. Not till man, the sinner, should master the profound and wondrous lessons contained in that book could the veil be removed and access granted. Not till He had come, who was to be the living personal exhibition or incarnation of all these lessons, could the sinner draw nigh to God.

It seemed a long time to wait, but it could not be otherwise. The lesson to be taught was a lesson not for Israel merely, but for the world; not for a few ages, but for eternity; not for earth only, but for heaven.

Every fresh sacrifice offered outside the veil was a new knock for admission, and a new cry, "How long, O Lord, how long." In patience the Old Testament saints waited on; assured that sooner or later the veil would rend or be swept away, and the way into the holiest be made manifest; the right of entrance to the mercy-seat seemed to the sinner for ever.

[6] Literally, "dying thou shalt die,"--that is, "thou shalt commence dying"; life with thee is at an end. Thus man was made to live, he was made immortal; it was sin that brought in mortality.

Chapter 3

The Symbolic Veil

The veil of the tabernacle was hung between the holy place and the holiest of all. Inside of it were the Ark of the Covenant, the mercy-seat, and the cherubim; outside were the golden altar of incense, the golden candlestick, or lamp-stand, and the table of shew- bread or "presence-bread," the twelve loaves that were placed before Jehovah.

Properly there were three veils or curtains for the tabernacle.

The outermost hung at the entrance of the tabernacle; and was always drawn aside, or might be so by any Israelite that wished to pass into the outer court, where the brazen altar and brazen laver were. That veil hindered no one, and concealed nothing. It was an ever-open door; at which any Israelite might come in with his sacrifice. It was at this door that the priest met the comer and examined his sacrifice to see if it were without blemish; for no blemished offering could pass the threshold; and the bringer of a blemished sacrifice must go back unaccepted and unblest. The Priest rejected him and his victim. He must go and get another bullock, or else bear his own sin.[7]

The second veil hung at the entrance of the holy place. It allowed any one to look in; but it prohibited the entrance of all but Priests. "Now when these things were thus ordained (arranged or set up) the priests went always (were continually going) into the first tabernacle (what we usually call the second), accomplishing the service of God" (Heb 9:6). They fed at the royal table there; they kept the lamps burning; they put incense on the golden altar. But they could enter no farther. The way into the holiest was not yet opened; the time had not yet come when the three places should be made one; all veils removed; all exclusions cancelled; all sprinkled with one blood; open freely to each coming one: altar, laver, table, candlestick, incense-altar, ark, and mercy-seat no longer separated, but brought together as being but parts of one glorious whole; divided from each other for a season, for the sake of distinct teaching and for the exhibition of sacrificial truth in its different parts and aspects; but in the fulness of time brought together;

as being but one perfect picture of the one perfect sacrifice, by means of which we have access to God and re-entrance into the Paradise which we had lost.

The third veil hung before the holy of holies: hiding, as it were, God from man and man from God, and intimating that the day of full meeting and fellowship had not yet come. It said to Israel, and it said to man (for all these things had a world-wide meaning), God is within; but you cannot enter now. The time is coming; but it is not yet.

In heathen temples there were veils hiding their holy places. But these pointed to no coming manifestation; no future unveiling of Him who was supposed to dwell within. These veils were but parts of the idolatry and darkness of the system; not proclamations of truth or promises of light. It was not so in the tabernacle. The veil that hid the glory was a promise of the revelation of that glory. In pagan shrines it was a signal of distress and despair; man's declaration that there was no hope of light; that the unknown must always be the unknown; nay, that the unknown was also the unknowable; and that the unapproached was also the unapproachable. In Israel's shrine the veil was a thing of light, not of darkness; it was a covering, no doubt, but it was also a revelation. It told what God was; where God was, and how God could be approached.

That it was not a gate,--of iron or brass, of silver or of gold,-- said much; that it was a veil of needlework, slight and moveable, said more. For it intimated that the hindrance in the way of the worshipper's nearer approach was slender and temporary. The nature of a tent intimated among other things its removeableness: "mine age is departed, and is removed from me as a shepherd's tent" (Isa 38:12). The nature of a veil in a tent intimates still greater slightness and removeableness. It was a thing which could easily be drawn aside, nay, which was, at the needed season, to be taken away. It was no wall of obstruction, but simply of temporary separation and exclusion, to be done away with in due time.

But while it was slight it was very beautiful. It is thus described:-- "And thou shalt make a veil of blue, and purple, and scarlet, and fine-twined linen, of cunning work: with cherubims shall it be made: and thou shalt hang it upon four pillars of shittim wood, overlaid with gold: their hooks shall be of gold upon the four sockets of silver" (Exo 26:31,32). Of the veil made by Solomon for the temple on Moriah it is said, "He made the veil of blue, and purple, and crimson, and fine linen, and wrought cherubims thereon" (2 Chron 3:14).

The temple-veil seems to have been thicker and of course larger every way, than that of the tabernacle. It is said to have been about twenty feet in height, and as much in width, strongly wrought and finely woven. It was never drawn, or at least only so much of it was moved aside once a-year as to admit the High Priest, when he approached the mercy-seat with blood and incense. For ages it stretched across that awful entrance, a more immoveable barrier than brass or iron: no Priest, or Levite, or Israelite venturing within its folds. Torn down again and again in different centuries, by the Babylonian, Persian, Grecian, and Roman invader, it was often replaced, that it might hang there, to teach its wondrous lessons, till God's great purpose with it had been fulfilled.

To the Jew of old there must have seemed something mysterious about that veil. It was not hung up merely to conceal what was within, as if God grudged to man the full vision of His glory, or had no desire to be approached. Many things connected with its texture and place showed that this was not the case. The unspiritual Jew of course was very likely to misjudge its use and import; and the historian Josephus is a specimen of that class. He seems to have had not the most distant idea of its use.[8] But the Israelite who had discernment in the things of God would see something far higher and nobler than this, though he might not understand it fully in connection with Messiah. Still he would see in that veil something glorious; something which both attracted and repelled; something which hid and revealed; something which spoke of himself and of his Messiah; for he knew that every thing pertaining to that tabernacle, and specially these on which cherubim were wrought, had reference to Messiah the Deliver, the seed of the woman, the man with the bruised heel.

All the curtains of the tabernacle had more or less the same reference. For on all of them the same devices were wrought. "Thou shalt make the tabernacle with ten curtains of fine-twined linen, and blue, and purple, and scarlet: with cherubims of cunning work shalt thou make them" (Exo 26:1, 36:8). The cherubim- figure was to be seen everywhere. That mysterious device which was first placed in Paradise, and which for ages had disappeared, was now reproduced in connection with the tabernacle. Since the garden of the Lord had been swept away (probably at the flood), the cherubim had not been seen; though doubtless tradition had handed down the memory of their appearance, and to Israel they were not strangers. Moses is now commanded to restore them. From Noah to Moses the Church had been a wanderer, with no sanctuary, only an altar to worship at. Yet, doubtless, Abraham, Isaac, and Jacob knew well about the cherubim; and when Moses was instructed to replace them he does not require to have their nature explained. They are now to be inwoven into the sanctuary,--that sanctuary which symbolised nothing less than Messiah Himself; teaching us that (whatever these cherubim might mean) the cherubim and Messiah were all "of one." The Church is represented in the tabernacle as one with Christ, "members of His body, of His flesh, and of His bones." Israel was taught that "the Church in the wilderness" (Acts 7:38) was as truly the body of Christ as the Church at Pentecost.

But however vague might be the ideas of the old Jew regarding the veil, it could not but be viewed as very peculiar, something by itself; part of the tabernacle furniture no doubt, yet a singular and unique part of it; in texture, in position, and in use, quite peculiar: exquisite as a piece of workmanship,--every colour and thread of which it was composed being symbolic and vocal. But still it was the frailest part of the fabric,--a strange contrast, in after days when the temple was built, with the massive marble walls and cedar beams, with which it was surrounded. For the temple was in all respects magnificent,-- even as a piece of architecture. Its enormous foundations were let in to the solid rock; its vast stones, each in itself a wall, rose tier above tier; its gates were of solid brass, so weighty, that one of them required twenty men to open and shut it. It thus presented a solid mass to view more like a part of the mountain than a mere building upon it.

But the veil was a thing which a child's hand could draw aside; and it was hung just where we should have expected a gate of brass or a wall of granite,-- at the entrance into the holiest of all,--to guard against the possibility of intrusion. Its frail texture in the midst of so much that was strong and massive, said that it was but a temporary barrier,--a screen,--in due time to be removed. The worshipper in the outer court, as he looked towards it from the outer entrance of the holy place, would see something of its workmanship, and might perhaps get some glimpses of the glory within shining through its folds. He would learn this much, at least, that the way into the holiest was not fully opened; yet it was only stopped by a veil, no more. He would conclude within himself, that though shut out now he would one day be allowed to enter and worship at the mercy-seat, or at something better than that mercy-seat, at the heavenly throne, in the true tabernacle which the Lord pitched, and not man, when the High Priest of good things to come should arrive, and as his forerunner, lead him into the very presence of that Invisible Jehovah who was now by symbols showing how He was to be approached and worshipped.

The veil! It hid God from man; for till that should be done which would make "grace reign through righteousness" (Rom 5:21), man could not be allowed to see God face to face. It hid man from God; for till this "righteousness" was established by the substitution of the just for the unjust, God could not directly look upon man. It hid the glory of God from man; it hid the shame of man from God. It so veiled or shaded both the shame and the glory, that it was possible for God to be near man, and yet not to repel him; and it was possible for man to be near God and yet not to be consumed.

The veil! It was let down from above, it did not spring up from below. It originated in God, and not in man. It was not man hiding himself from God, but God hiding Himself from man, as His holiness required, until it should become a right for a holy God and unholy man to meet each other in peace and love.

And it was sprinkled with blood! For though the expression "before the veil" (Lev 4:6) does not necessarily mean that it was sprinkled on the veil, yet the likelihood is that this was done. "The seven times, (says a commentator on Leviticus), throughout all Scripture, intimates a complete and perfect action. The blood is to be thoroughly exhibited before the Lord; life openly exhibited as taken, to honour the law that had been violated. It is not at this time taken within the veil; for that would require the priest to enter the holy of holies, a thing permitted only once a year. But it is taken very near the mercy- seat; it is taken 'before the veil,' while the Lord that dwelt between the cherubim bent down to listen to the cry that came up from the sin-atoning blood. Was the blood sprinkled on the veil? Some say not; but only on the floor close to the veil. The floor of the holy place was dyed with blood; a threshold of blood was formed, over which the High Priest must pass into on the day of judgment, when he entered into the most holy, drawing aside the veil. It is blood that opens our way into the presence of God; it is the voice of atoning blood that prevails with Him who dwells within. Others, however, with more probability, think that the blood was sprinkled on the veil. It might intimate that atonement was yet to rend that veil; and as that beautiful veil represented our Saviour's holy humanity (Heb 10:20), oh, how expressive was the continual repetition of the 'blood-sprinkling' seven times. As often as the Priest offered a sin-offering, the veil was wet again with blood, which dropped on the floor. Is this Christ bathed in the blood of atonement? Yes, through that veil the veil was opened to us, through the flesh of Jesus, through the body that for us was drenched in the sweat of blood."[9]

We speak of the blood-sprinkled mercy-seat, and the blood-sprinkled floor, on which that mercy-seat stood; but let us not forget the blood-sprinkled pavement, the "new and living way" into the holiest, and the blood-sprinkled veil. For "almost all things under the law were purged with blood, and without shedding of blood is no remission."

Nor let us forget Gethsemane, where "His sweat was as it were great drops of blood falling down to the ground." At His circumcision, at Gethsemane, at the cross, we see the blood-sprinkled veil. And all this for us; that the blood which was thus required at His hands should not be required of us.

[7] The true Priest,--"the High Priest of the good things to come"-- stands at the gate to receive all who come. He refuses none, however imperfect they and their offering may be; for it is His perfection and His perfect offering that give the right of entrance to the sinner; He receives all comers. "Him that cometh to me I will in no wise cast out."

[8] "The veils, which were composed of four things, declared the four elements; for the fine linen was proper to signify the earth, because the flax grows out of the earth; the purple signified the sea, because that colour is dyed by the blood of a sea shell-fish; the blue is fit to signify the air, and the scarlet will be an indication of fire."-- Antiq. b. iii. chap. 7. sect. 7.

[9] Dr. A. A. Bonar's Commentary on Leviticus, pp. 68, 69.

Chapter 4

The True Veil

All man's thoughts regarding the true meaning of the veil have been set at rest by that brief parenthesis of the Apostle Paul,-- "the veil, that is to say, His flesh" (Heb 10:20). The Holy Spirit has interpreted the symbol for us, and saved us a world of speculation and uncertainty. We now know that the veil meant the body of "Jesus."[10]

Thus Christ is seen in every part of the tabernacle; and everywhere it is the riches of His grace that we see. Here "Christ is all and in all." The whole fabric is Christ. Each separate part is Christ. The altar is Christ the sacrifice. The laver is Christ filled with the Spirit for us. The curtains speak of Him. The entrances all speak of Him. Candlestick, and table, and golden altar speak of Him. The Ark of the Covenant, the mercy-seat, the glory, all embody and reveal Him. Everything here says, "Behold the Lamb of God who taketh away the sin of the world."

But the veil is "His flesh,"--His body, His humanity. As the lamb was to be without blemish, and without spot, in order to set forth His perfection; so the veil was perfect in all its parts, finely wrought and beautiful to the eye, to exhibit the excellency of Him who is fairer than the children of men. As the veil was composed of the things of earth, so was His body; not only bone of our bone and flesh of His flesh, but nourished in all its parts by the things of earth, fed by the things which grew out of the soil, as we are fed. Christ's flesh was perfect, though earthly: without sin, though of the substance of a sinful woman; unblemished in every part, yet sensitive to all our sinless infirmities. Through the veil the glory shone, so through the body of Christ the Godhead shone.

As in the holy of holies the shekinah or symbol of Jehovah dwelt; so in the man Christ Jesus dwelt "all the fulness of the Godhead BODILY" (Col 2:9). He was "the Word made flesh" (John 1:14); "God manifest in flesh" (1 Tim 3:16); "Immanuel," God with us; Jehovah in very deed dwelling on earth, inhabiting a temple made with hands; and that temple a human body such as ours. For God became man that He might dwell with man, and that man might dwell with Him. In Jesus of Nazareth Jehovah was manifested; so that he who saw Him saw the Father, and he who heard Him heard the Father, and he who knew Him knew the Father.

In Jesus of Nazareth was seen the mighty God. In the son of the carpenter was seen the Creator of heaven and earth. In the Man of sorrows was seen the Son of the blessed. He who was born at Bethlehem was He whose days are from eternity. He who died was the Prince of life, of whom it is written, "In Him was life, and the life was the light of men." Of these things the mysterious veil of the temple was the fair symbol. He who could read the meaning of that veil could read unutterable things concerning the coming Messiah,--the Redeemer of His Israel, the Deliverer of man; divine yet human, heavenly yet earthly, clothed with divine majesty, yet wearing the raiment of our poor humanity.

In Him was manifested divine strength, residing in and working through a feeble human arm such as ours: divine wisdom, in its perfection, speaking through the lips of a child of dust; divine majesty seated on a human brow; divine benignity beaming from human eyes, and put forth in the touch of a human hand; divine purposes working themselves out through a human will; divine sovereignty embodied in each act and motion of a human organism; divine grace coming forth in human compassions and sympathies; and divine grief finding vent to itself in human tears.

The perfection of His holy and glorious, yet true manhood is seen in that mysterious veil. Its materials, so choice, so fair, yet still earthly, spoke of Him who, though fairer than the children of men, is still bone of our bone and flesh of our flesh. Its well-wrought texture and exquisite workmanship, of purple, and scarlet, and fine-twined linen, spoke of His spotless yet thoroughly human body, prepared by the Holy Ghost; while its embroidered or interwoven cherubim spoke of the Church in Him,--part of Himself; one with Him as He is one with them; for "both He that sanctifieth and they who are sanctified are all of one."

The "flesh of Christ" both revealed and hid the glory. It veiled and it unveiled Godhead: it proclaimed the nearness of Jehovah to His worshippers, and yet suggested some distance, some interposing medium, which could only be taken out of the way by God Himself. For that which had been placed there by God could not be removed by man. And yet man, in a certain sense, had to do with the removal. In the type, indeed, it was not so; but in the antitype it was. For no hand of man rent the veil; yet it was man's hand that nailed the Son of God to the cross; it was man that slew Him. And yet again, on the other hand, it was God that smote Him,--just as it was the hand of God that rent the veil from top to bottom. "It pleased the Lord to bruise Him and to put Him to grief" (Isa 53:10). The bruising of His heel was the doing of the serpent and his seed, yet it was also the doing of the Lord.

There was the unbroken body, and the broken body of the Lord. The veil pointed to the former. It was the symbol of the unbroken body, the unwounded flesh of the Surety. It was connected with incarnation, not with crucifixion,--with life, not with death. We learn from it that mere incarnation can do nothing for the sinner. He needs far more than that,--something different from the mere assumption of our humanity. The veil said, that body must be broken before the sinner can come as a worshipper into the place where Jehovah dwells. The Christ of God must not merely take flesh and blood; He must take mortal flesh and die. Sacrifice alone can bring us nigh to God, and keep us secure and blessed in His presence. We are saved by a dying Christ.

The veil was, as we have said before, to the holy of holies what the sword of fire was to the garden of the Lord. Both of them kept watch at the gate of the divine presence-chamber. The flaming sword turned every way; that is, it threw around the garden a girdle or belt of divine fire from the shekinah glory, threatening death to all who should seek entrance into the holiest, and yet (by leaving Paradise unscathed upon the earth) revealing God's gracious purpose of preserving it for the re-entrance of banished man, or rather of preparing for him a home more glorious than the Paradise which he had lost.

Both the veil and the flame said, "We guard the palace of the Great King, that no sinner may enter." Yet they said also, the King is within, He has not forsaken man or man's world; you shall one day have unhindered access to Him; but for wise and vast reasons, to be shown in due time, you cannot enter yet. Something must be done to make your entrance a safe thing for yourself and a righteous thing for God.

That veil then, unrent as it was, proclaimed the glad tidings; though it could not, so long as it was unrent, reveal the whole grace, or at least the way in which grace is to reach the sinner. That grace can flow out only by means of death. It is death that opens the pent-up fulness of love, and sends out the life contained in the "spring shut up, the fountain sealed." It is the rod of the substitute, the cross of the sin-bearer that smites the rock, that the waters may gush forth.

The antitype of the unrent veil might be said to have been held before Israel's eyes from the time that the Son of God took our flesh. It is the unrent veil that we find at Bethlehem; it is the unrent veil that we find at Nazareth, and all the life long of the Christ of God. The miracles of grace wrought during His ministry were like the waving of the folds of that veil before men's eyes, and letting some of the rays of the inner majesty shine through. So were His words of grace from day to day. Men were compelled to look and to admire. "They wondered at the gracious words proceeding out of His mouth" (Luke 4:22, literally, "at the words of the grace proceeding out of His mouth"); "Never man spake like this man" (John 7:46); "He hath done all things well" (Mark 7:37); what were these things but the expressions of admiration at the unrent veil. It was so beautiful, so perfect! Men gazed at it and wondered. It was marvellously attractive; and it was meant to be so.

Hence many were drawn to the person of Christ by His attractive grace without fully understanding either His fulness or their own great need. What they saw in a living Christ won their hearts; they acknowledged Him as the Saviour without fully understanding how He was to be such. The disciples would not admit any necessity for His dying. The unrent veil seemed to them enough. "That be far from Thee, Lord," were the words of Peter, repudiating the very idea of His Lord's death. He was content with a living Saviour. Death seemed altogether inconsistent with the character of Messiah.

Let us mark the scene just referred to, and understand its meaning. "From that time forth began Jesus to show unto His disciples, how that He must go to Jerusalem, and suffer many things of the elders and chief priests and scribes, and be killed and be raised again the third day" (Matt 16:21). It was as if standing in front of the holy of holies, and pointing to the veil, He was saying to them, That veil must be rent! "Then Peter took Him, and began to rebuke him, saying, Be it far from Thee, Lord; this shall not be unto Thee" (v 22). What was this but saying, Lord, that is impossible; that veil must not and cannot be rent! "But He turned and said unto Peter, Get thee behind me, Satan; thou art an offence unto me; for thou savourest not the things that be of God, but those that be of men" (v 23). It was as if He had said, Peter, thou art speaking like Satan, and for Satan; he knows that unless the heel of the woman's seed be bruised, his head cannot be bruised; he knows that unless that veil be rent, thou canst not go in to God; and he speaks through thee, if it were possible, to prevent the rending; the veil must be rent; if I die not, thou canst not live; if I die not, I need not have come into the world at all.[11]

If one might, by a figure, speak of the veil as living and sentient, might we not say that it dreaded the rending. What was the meaning of Christ's words, "Now is my soul sorrowful"? Was it not the expression of dread as to the rending? And still more, what was the meaning of the Gethsemane cry, "Father, if it be Thy will, let this cup pass from me"? Was it not the same? And yet there was the desire for its being rent, the longing for the consummation. "I have a baptism to be baptized with, and how am I straitened till it be accomplished" (Luke 12:50).

"A body hast thou prepared me" (Heb 10:5). That body was truly human as we have seen, and yet it was prepared by the Holy Ghost. "The Holy Ghost shall come upon thee, and the power of the Highest shall overshadow thee; therefore also,[12] that holy thing which shall be born of thee shall be called the Son of God" (Luke 1:35). This body, thus divinely prepared out of human materials, was altogether wonderful. There had been none like it from the first: nor was there to be any such after it,--so perfect, yet so thoroughly human; so stainless, yet so sensitive to all the sinless infirmities of man. In this respect it differed from the body of the first Adam, which was perfect, no doubt, but not in sympathy with us. The kind of perfection in the first Adam unfitted him to sympathise with us, or to be tempted like as we are. The nature of Christ's perfection fitted Him most fully for sympathising with us, and for being tempted, like as we are, yet without sin.

The colour and texture of the temple-veil seem all to have reference to the flesh or body; blue, and purple, and scarlet, and fine-twined linen. Jeremiah's description of the Nazarites may help us to see this: "Her Nazarites were purer than snow, they were whiter than milk; they were more ruddy in body than rubies; their polishing was of sapphire" (Lam 4:7, or "their veining was the sapphire's," as Blayney renders it). The bride in the Song of Solomon thus also speaks of the bridegroom, "My beloved is white and ruddy, the chiefest among ten thousand" (Song of Sol 5:10).

All this corporeal perfection and beauty were produced by the Holy Ghost. Never had His hand brought forth such material perfection as in the body of the Christ of God. It was "without spot and blemish," worthy of Him out of whose eternal purpose it came forth; worthy of Him who so cunningly had wrought it as the perfection of divine workmanship; worthy of Him in whom dwelt all the fulness of the Godhead bodily.[13]

[10] In the previous verse he had spoken of the "blood of Jesus,"--so here we understand him to say that the veil is the body of Him whose name is Jesus; that one name at which every knee shall bow: that one name of which all prophecy is the testimony (Rev 19:10). In the above passage, in Philippians, it is very noticeable that JESUS by itself should be so specially singled out; JESUS as the special name for worship and for worshippers. "In the name of Jesus every knee shall bow." Of all His many names this is the one which the Father delights to honour, and round which the eternal adoration of heaven and earth is to gather. It is the name of names:--the name above every name,--JESUS.

[11] Christ's calling Peter by the name of Satan, and thus identifying him, in what he had just been saying, with the old tempter, carries us back to the first promise, in which that tempter heard his own doom and man's deliverance predicted. If Jesus did not die, if the heel of the woman's seed were not bruised, the first promise fell to the ground. Satan knew how much turned upon the bruising of the heel of that seed, and how necessary it was to the bruising of his own head. Nothing could have more identified Peter with Satan than the position he took up here as to the non- necessity for his Master's death. Nicodemus did not understand the person of the Lord; Peter did not understand His work, nor see the necessity for His sacrificial death.

[12] "Therefore even that which shall be born shall be holy; it shall be called the Son of God."

[13] Dr. Owen dwells at length upon this point, the forming of Christ's body by the Holy Spirit. "The framing, forming, and miraculous conception of the body of Christ, in the womb of the blessed virgin, was the peculiar and special work of the Holy Ghost...It was effected by an act of infinite creating power, yet it was formed or made of the substance of the blessed virgin."--On the Holy Spirit, b. ii. chap. 3.

Chapter 5

The Rending of the Veil

The symbolic veil was rent: and at the same moment the true veil was also rent. It is this that we have now to consider.

The following are the words of the evangelist: "Behold the veil of the temple was rent in twain from the top to the bottom" (Matt 27:51). In considering them we must endeavour to realise the scene of which this is a part. The passage transports us to Jerusalem; it sets us down upon Moriah; it takes us into the old temple at the hour of evening sacrifice, when the sun, though far down the heavens, is still sending its rays right over turret and pinnacle, on to the grey slopes of Olivet, where thousands, gathered for the great Paschal Sacrifice, are wandering; it shows us the holy chambers with their varied furniture of marble and cedar and gold; it brings us into the midst of the ministering priests, all robed for service. Then suddenly, as through the opened sky, it lifts us up and carries us from the earthly into the heavenly places, from the mortal into the immortal Jerusalem, of which it is written by one who had gazed upon them both, "I saw no temple therein, for the Lord God Almighty and the Lamb are the temple of it."

For we must take the earthly and the heavenly together, as body and soul. The terrestrial sun and the sun of righteousness must mingle their radiance, and each unfold the other. The waters of the nether and the upper springs must flow together. The Church must be seen in Israel, and Israel in the Church; Christ in the altar, and the altar in Christ; Christ in the lamb, and the lamb in Christ; Christ in the mercy-seat, and the mercy-seat in Christ; Christ in the shekinah-glory, and the shekinah-glory in Him, who is the brightness of Jehovah's glory. We must not separate the shadow from the substance, the material from the spiritual, the visible form the invisible glory. What God hath joined together, let no man put asunder.

Even the old Jew, if a believing man, like Simeon, saw these two things together, though in a way and order and proportion considerably different from what our faith now realises. To him there was the vision of the heavenly through the earthly; to us there is the vision of the earthly through the heavenly. He, standing on the outside, saw the glory through the veil, as one in a valley sees the sunshine through clouds; we, placed in the inside, see the veil through the glory, as one far up the mountain sees the clouds beneath through the sunshine. Formerly it was the earthly that revealed the heavenly, now it is the heavenly that illuminates the earthly. Standing beside the brazen serpent, Moses might see afar off Messiah the Healer of the nations; standing, or rather I should say sitting, by faith beside this same Messiah in the heavenly places, we see the brazen serpent afar off. From the rock of Horeb, the elders of Israel might look up and catch afar off some glimpses of the water of life flowing from the rock of ages; we, close by the heavenly fountain, proceeding out of the throne of God and of the Lamb, look down and recognise the old desert rock, with its gushing stream. Taking in his hand the desert manna, Israel could look up to the true bread above; we, taking into our hands the bread of God, look downward on the desert manna, not needing now with Israel to ask, "What is it?"

But let us look at

The rending of the veil. This was a new thing in its history, and quite a thing fitted to make Israel gaze and wonder, and ask, what meaneth this? Is Jehovah about to forsake His dwelling?

1. It was rent, not consumed by fire. For not its mere removal, still less its entire destruction, was to be signified; but its being transformed from being a barrier into a gate of entrance. Through it the way into the holiest was to pass; the new and living way; over a pavement sprinkled with blood.

2. It was rent while the temple stood. Had the earthquake which rent the rocks and opened graves, struck down the temple or shattered its walls, men might have said that it was this that rent the veil. But now was it made manifest that it was no earthly hand, nor natural convulsion, that was thus throwing open the mercy-seat, and making its long-barred chamber as entirely accessible as the wide court without, which all might enter, and where all might worship.

3. It was rent in twain. It did not fall to pieces, nor was it torn in pieces. The rent was a clean and straight one, made by some invisible hand; and the exact division into two parts might well figure the separation of Christ's soul and body, while each part remained connected with the temple, as both body and soul remained in union with the Godhead; as well as resemble the throwing open of the great folding

door between earth and heaven, and the complete restoration of the fellowship between God and man.

4. It was rent from the top to the bottom. Not from side to side, nor from the bottom to the top: which might have been man's doing; but from the top to the bottom, showing that the power which rent it was from above, not from beneath; that the rending was not of man but of God. It was man, no doubt, that dealt the blow of death to the Son of God, but, "it pleased the Lord to bruise him; He hath put him to grief." Beginning with the roof and ending with the floor, the rest was complete; for God, out of His own heaven, had done it. And as from roof to floor there remained not one fragment of the old veil; so from heaven to earth, from the throne of God, down to the dwelling of man, there exists not one remnant nor particle of a barrier between the sinner and God. He who openeth and no man shutteth has, with His own hand, and in His own boundless love, thrown wide open to the chief of sinners, the innermost recesses of His own glorious heaven! Let us go in: let us draw near.

5. It was rent in the presence of the priests. They were in the holy place, outside the veil, of course, officiating, lighting the lamps, or placing incense on the golden altar, or ordering the shewbread on the golden table. They saw the solemn rending of the veil, and were no doubt overwhelmed with amazement; ready to flee out of the place, or to cover their eyes lest they should see the hidden glories of that awful chamber which only one was permitted to behold. "Woe is me, for I am undone; I am a man of unclean lips, and I dwell among a people of unclean lips; for mine eyes have seen the King, the Lord of Hosts" (Isa 6:5). They were witnesses of what was done. They had not done it themselves; they felt that no mortal hand had done it; and what could they say but that God Himself had thrown open His gates, that they might enter in to precincts from which they had been so long debarred.

6. It was rent that it might disclose the mercy- seat, and the cherubim, and the glory. These were no longer to be hidden, and known only as the mysterious occupants of a chamber from which they might not go out, and into which no man might enter. It was no longer profanity to handle the uncovered vessels of the inner shrine; to gaze upon the golden floor and walls all stained with sacrificial blood; nay, to go up to the mercy-seat and sit down beneath the very shadow of the glory. Formerly it was blasphemy even to speak of entering in; now the invitation seemed all at once to go forth, "Let us come boldly to the throne of grace." The safest, as well as the most blessed place, is beneath the shadow of the glory.

7. It was rent at the time of the evening sacrifice. About three o'clock, when the sun began to go down, the lamb was slain, and laid upon the brazen altar. Just at the moment when its blood was shed, and the smoke arose from the fire that was consuming it, the veil was rent in twain. There was an unseen link between the altar and the veil, between the sacrifice and the rending, between the bloodshedding and the removal of the barrier. It was blood that had done the work. It was blood that had rent the veil and thrown open the mercy-seat: the blood of "the Lamb, without blemish, and without spot."

8. It was rent at the moment when the Son of God died on the cross. His death, then, had done it! Nay, more, that rending and that death were one thing; the one a symbol, the other a reality; but both containing one lesson, that LIFE was the screen which stood between us and God, and death the removal of the screen; that it was His death that made His incarnation available for sinners; that it was from the cross of Golgotha that the cradle of Bethlehem derived all its value and its virtue; that the rock of ages, like the rock of Rephidim, must be smitten before it can become a fountain of living waters. That death was like the touching of the electric wire between Calvary and Moriah, setting loose suddenly the divine power that for a thousand years had been lying in wait to rend the veil and cast down the barrier. It was from the cross that the power emanated which rent the veil. From that place of weakness and shame and agony, came forth the omnipotent command, "Lift up your heads, O ye gates, and be ye lifted up, ye everlasting doors." The "It is finished" upon Golgotha was the appointed signal, and the instantaneous response was the rending of the veil. Little did the Jew think, when nailing the Son of the carpenter to the tree, that it was these pierced hands that were to rend the veil, and that it was their being thus pierced that fitted them for this mysterious work. Little did he suppose, when erecting a cross for the Nazarene, that that cross was to be the lever by which both his temple and city were to be razed to their foundations. Yet so it was. It was the cross of Christ that rent the veil; overthrew the cold statutes of symbolic service; consecrated the new and living way into the holiest; supplanted the ritualistic with the real and the true; and substituted for lifeless performances the living worship of the living God.

9. When the veil was rent, the cherubim which were embroidered on it were rent with it. And as these cherubim symbolised the Church of the redeemed, there was thus signified our identification with Christ in His death. We were nailed with Him to the cross; we were crucified with Him; with Him we died, and were buried, and rose

again. In that rent veil we have the temple-symbol of the apostle's doctrine, concerning oneness with Christ in life and death,-- "I am crucified with Christ." And in realising the cross and the veil, let us realise these words of solemn meaning, "Ye are dead, and your life is hid with Christ in God."

The broken body and shed blood of the Lord had at length opened the sinner's way into the holiest. And these were the tokens not merely of grace, but of righteousness. That rending was no act either of mere power or of mere grace. Righteousness had done it. Righteousness had rolled away the stone. Righteousness had burst the gates of brass, and cut in sunder the bars of iron. It was a righteous removal of the barrier; it was a righteous entrance that had been secured for the unrighteous; it was a righteous welcome for the chief of sinners that was now proclaimed.

Long had the blood of bulls and goats striven to rend the veil, but in vain. Long had they knocked at the awful gate, demanding entrance for the sinner; long had they striven to quench the flaming sword, and unclasp the fiery belt that girdled paradise; long had they demanded entrance for the sinner, but in vain. But now the better blood has come; it knocks but once, and the gate flies open; it but once touches the sword of fire, and it is quenched. Not a moment is lost. The fulness of the time has come. God delays not, but unbars the door at once. He throws open His mercy-seat to the sinner, and makes haste to receive the banished one; more glad even than the wanderer himself that the distance, and the exclusion, and the terror are at an end for ever.

O wondrous power of the cross of Christ! To exalt the low, and to abase the high; to cast down and to build up; to unlink and to link; to save and to destroy; to kill and to make alive; to shut out and to let in; to curse and to bless. O wondrous virtue of the saving cross, which saves in crucifying, and crucifies in saving! For four thousand years has paradise been closed, but Thou hast opened it. For ages and generations the presence of God has been denied to the sinner, but Thou hast given entrance,-- and that not timid, and uncertain, and costly, and hazardous; but bold, and blessed, and safe, and free.

The veil, then, has been rent in twain from the top to the bottom. The way is open, the blood is sprinkled, the mercy-seat is accessible to all, and the voice of the High Priest, seated on that mercy- seat, summons us to enter, and to enter without fear. Having, then, boldness to enter into the holiest by the blood of Jesus,--by a new and living way which He hath consecrated for us, through the veil, that is to say, His flesh, and having an High Priest over the house of God, let us draw near with a true heart, in the full assurance of faith. The message is, Go in, go in. Let us respond to the message, and at once draw near. To stand afar off, or even upon the threshhold, is to deny and dishonour the provision made for our entrance, as well as to incur the awful peril of remaining outside the one place of safety or blessedness. To enter in is our only security and our only joy. But we must go in in a spirit and attitude becoming the provision made for us. If that provision has been insufficient, we must come hesitatingly, doubtingly, as men who can only venture on an uncertain hope of being welcomed. If the veil be not wholly rent, if the blood be not thoroughly sprinkled, or be in itself insufficient, if the mercy-seat be not wholly what its name implies,--a seat of mercy, a throne of grace; if the High Priest be not sufficiently compassionate and loving, or if there be not sufficient evidence that these things are so, the sinner may come doubtingly and uncertainly; but if the veil be fully rent, and the blood be of divine value and potency, and the mercy-seat be really the place of grace, and the High Priest full of love to the sinner, then every shadow of a reason for doubt is swept utterly away. Not to come with the boldness is the sin. Not to come in the full assurance of faith is the presumption. To draw near with an "evil conscience" is to declare our belief that the blood of the Lamb is not of itself enough to give the sinner a good conscience and a fearless access.

"May I then draw near as I am, in virtue of the efficacy of the sprinkled blood?" Most certainly. In what other way or character do you propose to come? And may I be bold at once? Most certainly. For if not at once, then when and how? Let boldness come when it may, it will come to you from the sight of the blood upon the floor and mercy-seat, and from nothing else. It is bold coming that honours the blood. It is bold coming that glorifies the love of God and the grace of His throne. "Come boldly!" this is the message to the sinner. Come boldly now! Come in the full assurance of faith, not supposing it possible that that God who has provided such a mercy-seat can do anything but welcome you; that such a mercy-seat can be anything to you but the place of pardon, or that the gospel out of which every sinner that has believed it has extracted peace, can contain anything but peace to you.

The rent veil is liberty of access. Will you linger still? The sprinkled blood is boldness,-- boldness for the sinner, for any sinner, for every sinner. Will you still hesitate, tampering and dallying with uncertainty and doubt, and an evil conscience? Oh, take that blood for what it is and gives, and go in. Take that rent veil for what it indicates, and go in. This only will make you a peaceful, happy, holy man. This only will enable you to work for God on earth, unfettered and unburdened; all over joyful, all over loving, and all over free. This will make your religion not that of one who has everything yet to settle between himself and God, and whose labours, and duties, and devotions are all undergone for the purpose of working out that momentous adjustment before life shall close, but the religion of one who, having at the very outset, and simply in believing, settled every question between himself and God over the blood of the Lamb, is serving the blessed One who has loved him and bought him, with all the undivided energy of his liberated and happy soul.

For every sinner, without exception, that veil has a voice, that blood a voice, that mercy-seat a voice. They say, "Come in." They say, "Be reconciled to God." They say, "Draw near." They say, "Seek the Lord while He may be found." To the wandering prodigal, the lover of pleasure, the drinker of earth's maddening cup, the dreamer of earth's vain dreams,--they say, there is bread enough in your Father's house, and love enough in your Father's heart, and to spare,--return, return. To each banished child of Adam, exiles from the paradise which their first father lost, these symbols, with united voice, proclaim the extinction of the fiery sword, the re- opening of the long-barred gate, with a free and abundant re-entrance, or rather, entrance into a more glorious paradise, a paradise that was never lost.

But if all these voices die away unheeded,--if you will not avail yourself, O man, of that rent veil, that open gate,--what remains but the eternal exclusion, the hopeless exile, the outer darkness, where there is the weeping and wailing and gnashing of teeth? Instead of the rent veil, there shall be drawn the dark curtain, never to be removed or rent, which shall shut you out from God, and from paradise, and from the New Jerusalem for ever. Instead of the mercy- seat, there comes the throne of judgment; and instead of the gracious High Priest, there comes the avenging Judge. Yes, the Lord Jesus Christ is coming, and with His awful advent ends all thy hope. He is coming; and He may be nearer than you think. In an hour when you are not aware He will come. When you are saying peace and safety, He will come. When you are dreaming of earth's long, calm, summer days, He will come. Lose no time. Trifle no more with eternity; it is too long and too great to be trifled with. Make haste! Get these affections disengaged from a present evil world. Get these sins of thine buried in the grave of Christ. Get that soul of thine wrapped up, all over, in the perfection of the perfect One, in the righteousness of the righteous One. Then all is well, all is well. But till then thou hast not so much as one true hope for eternity or for time.

Chapter 6

The Removal of the First Sacrifice and the Establishment of the Second

The temple was not overthrown till about forty years after the Son of God died on the cross. The type was preserved for a season, that the antitype might be more fully understood. The shadow and the substance were thus for forty years exhibited together. The temple still, in its rites, proclaimed what the apostles preached. Every part of it spoke aloud and said, "Look on me, and look away from me; look to Him of whom I have been bearing witness for these many ages; behold the Lamb of God which taketh away the sin of the world."

But in God's sight the first sacrifice was finished when Jesus died. Then the purpose for which the blood had been shed day by day was accomplished.

Thus the apostle writes, "He taketh away the first that He may establish the second" (Heb 10:9).

To a Jew this language must have sounded strange, if not profane; quite as much so as did the words, "Destroy this temple, and in three days I will raise it up." A first and second what? Does he rightly hear the words?

Is it a second temple, a second altar, a second priesthood; the first being set aside? That cannot be! Israel's service is divine; it is one and unchanging. Messiah, when He comes, will confirm, not destroy it. Israel's service is a first without a second. A second is an impossibility, a blasphemy.

Yet the apostle, a Jew, writing to Jews, announces this incredible thing! He announces it as an indisputable certainty; and he expects to be believed. Had he announced a second sun or a second universe, rising out of the extinction of the first, he would not have been reckoned so outrageous in his statement as in declaring the abolition of Israel's present service, and the substitution of one more perfect, and no less divine.

Chapter 6

1. But what is this first? Speaking generally, it means the old temple and tabernacle service; the old covenant made with Israel in the desert, from Mount Sinai. But the special thing in this service to which he points is the sacrifice or sacrifices; the blood of bullocks and of goats, the morning and evening sacrifice of the lamb for the daily burnt- offering, in which all the other sacrifices were wrapt up,--which was the very heart and soul of all the worship carried on in that sanctuary.

2. By whom was this "first" taken away? By Him who set it up, and upheld it for so many ages; "He taketh away the first." He, the Lord God of Israel, the God of Abraham and Isaac and Jacob. It was not man who destroyed it, even as it was not man who established it. Long before the city was overthrown and the temple perished, the sacrifice had come to an end, the temple service had run its course.

3. When was it taken away? On that afternoon of the passover when the Son of God died upon the cross; that awful hour when the sun was darkened, and the earth shook, and the rocks were rent. Then, at eventide, at three o'clock, the last Jewish sacrifice was laid upon the brazen altar. In God's reckoning that was really the last. No doubt, for years after this sacrifices continued to be offered up; but these could no longer be said to be of divine appointment. The number of burnt-offerings according to God's purpose was now complete; their end had been served; they passed away. From the day that Solomon laid the first lamb on the temple altar; from the day that Moses laid the first on the tabernacle altar; from the day that Adam laid his first upon the altar at the gate of Paradise, how many tens of thousands had been offered! But now God's great purpose with them is served. All is done. The last of the long series has been laid upon the altar.

4. How was this first taken away? Simply by setting another in its place; making it give way to something better. Not by violence, or fire, or the sword of man. The altar sent up its last blaze that evening as brightly as ever. The blaze sank down, and all has since been dark. The great end was served; the great lesson taught; the great truth written down for man. Then and thus the fire ceased to burn, and the blood to flow. No more of such fire or such blood was needed. The first was taken away without the noise of axes or hammers, because its work was done.

5. For what end did He take away the first? That He might establish the second. The first seemed steadfast; Israel reckoned on it standing for ever; it had stood for many an age. Yet it gives way, and another comes: one meant to be more abiding than the first; one sacri-

fice, once for all; yet that sacrifice eternal; the same in its results on the worshipper as if it were offered up every day for ever; the basis and seal of the everlasting covenant. It was to make room for this glorious second that the first was taken away; this glorious second through which eternal redemption was accomplished for us.

Besides, it had come to be necessary, on other grounds, that the first should be taken away. It was beginning to defeat the very ends for which it was set up. Men were getting to look upon it as a real thing in itself; and to believe in it instead of believing in Him to whom it pointed. It was becoming an object of worship and of trust, as if it were the true propitiation; as if the blood of beasts could pacify the conscience, or reconcile God, or put away sin. It was becoming an idol; a substitute for the living God, and for His Christ, instead of showing the way of true approach and acceptable worship. As men in our day make an idol of their own faith, and believe in it instead of believing in the Son of God, so did the Jews of other days make the sacrifice their confidence, their resting-place, their Messiah. And as Hezekiah broke in pieces the brazen serpent when Israel began to worship it, so did God abolish the sacrifice.

That sacrifice was not in itself a real thing, nor did it accomplish anything real. It was but a picture, a statue, a shadow, a messenger,-- no more. It was but the sketch or outline of the living thing that was to come; and to mistake it for that living thing itself was to be deluded with the subtlest of all errors, and the most perilous of all idolatries. And what can be more dangerous for a soul than to mistake the unreal for the real; to dote upon the picture, and lose sight of the glorious Being represented? Ah, we do not thus deceive ourselves in earthly things! No man mistakes the picture of gold for gold itself, or the portrait of a loved face for the very face itself. Yet do we daily see how men are content with religious unrealities; the unrealities of a barren creed, or of a hollow form; the unrealities of doubt and uncertainty in the relationship between them and God. We find how many of those called religious men are satisfied with something far short of a living Christ, and a full assurance and a joyful hope.

Nay, they make this unreality of theirs an idol, a god; not venturing to step beyond it, not caring to part with it. They have become so familiar with it, that though it does not fill their soul, it soothes their uneasiness; it gratifies the religious element in their natural man; it pleases their self- righteousness, for it is something of their own; and it saves them from the dreaded necessity of coming into direct contact with the real, the living Christ, of being brought face to face with God Himself.

Thus it comes to pass that a man's religion is often a barrier between his soul and God; the unreal is the substitute for the real; so that a man, having found the former, is content, and goes no farther; nay, counts it presumption, profanity to do so. To be told that the world, with its gay beauty and seducing smiles, comes between us and God, surprises no man; but to learn that the temple with its sacrifices, the Church with its religious services, does so, may startle some, nay, may exasperate them, as it did the Jews, to be told that their multiplied sacrifices and prayers were but multiplied barriers between them and God: not channels of communication, nor means of intercourse. The Jewish altar stood between the Jew and God; and that which was simply set as the ladder up to something higher became a resting-place. All the more, because it looked so real to the eye; while that to which it pointed was invisible, and therefore to sense unreal. But real as it looked, it was cold and unsatisfying. It was a real lamb, and a real altar of solid stone and brass; it was real blood and fire and smoke; and to take away these might seem to take away all that was substantial. But, after all, these were the unrealities. They could accomplish nothing for the filling of the heart, or the pacifying of the conscience, or the healing of the soul's deep wounds. Yet they pointed to the real; and their very unreality was meant to keep man from making them his home, or his religion, or his god. Men might admire the holy symbols and majestic ritual; but the true use of such admiration was to lead them to reason thus, If the unreal be so attractive, what will the real be; if the shadow thus soothes and pleases, what will not the divine substance do; if the picture of Messiah, thus sketched in these ceremonies, be so fair and goodly, how much fairer and goodlier will be the living Christ Himself; if the porch of the temple, or the steps leading to that temple, be so excellent, what must the inner sanctuary be; and who would stand ths, all a lifetime, shivering in the cold without, when the whole interior, with all its warmth and splendour and life and vastness was thrown open, and every man invited to enter and partake the gladness?

Thus the "taking away of the first" was not the mere removal of what had done its work and become useless; but the abolition of that which had become an idol; a barrier between the Jew and God; quite as much as if the brazen altar had in the process of time become so enlarged as to block up the entrance into the holy place or the holiest of all. We read in Jewish history that once and again, during the seventeen sieges of Jerusalem, the gate of the temple was blocked up by the

dead bodies of the worshippers. So did the access into the true tabernacle, not made with hands, become blocked up by the very sacrifices
that were intended to point to the open door; and so in our day (long
after that altar has been overturned and the fire quenched), is entrance
into the holiest blocked up by our dead prayers, our dead works, our
dead praises, our dead sacraments, our dead worship, our dead religion, quite as effectually as by our total want of these. A lesson hard for
man to learn, especially in days when religion is fashionable and forms
are exalted above measure. Greatly is that text needed amongst us, "If
the blood of bulls and of goats and the ashes of an heifer sprinkling the
unclean, sanctifieth to the purifying of the flesh, how much more shall
the blood of Christ purge your conscience from dead works to serve
the living God?" (Heb 9:14).

It is then through the "second," not the "first," that the conscience is purged and the man made an acceptable worshipper, capable
of doing good works and doing them in the spirit of liberty and fearless gladness. It is with the second, not the first, that the sinner has to
do in drawing near to God; and it is the second, not the first, that God
has regard to in receiving the sinner, and receiving him on the footing
of one whose sins and iniquities are remembered no more.

How wide the difference, how great the contrast between the
first and the second! The first drew the veil and shut out the sinner
from the holiest; the second rent it and bid him enter. The first filled
the sinner's soul with dread, even in looking on the holiest of all from
without; the second emboldened him to draw near and go up to the
mercy-seat. The first made it death to cross the threshold of that inner
shrine, where the symbol of the glory dwelt; the second made it life to
go into the very presence of God, and provided the new and living
way. The first gave no certainty of acceptance and laid the foundation
for no permanent assurance; the second said, "Let us draw near with a
true heart in the full assurance of faith"; "let us come boldly to the
throne of grace." The first was never finished, even after many ages;
the second was finished at once. The first was earthly, the second
heavenly. The first was temporal, the second eternal. The first was unreal, the second real. The first pacified no conscience; the second did
this at once, purging it effectually, so that the worshippers once purged
had no more conscience of sins. The first was but the blood of one of
Israel's lambs; the second the blood of the Lamb without blemish and
without spot,--the precious blood of Christ!

Still there was much about that "first" to interest, to solemnise,
to gladden. It was old and venerable, a true relic of antiquity, such as

no modern Church can boast of. It was not one death, but many thousand deaths; not one victim, but ten thousand victims; each of them fulfilling a certain end, yet all of them unavailing for the great end,-- complete remission of sin and the providing for the worshipper, a perfect conscience and reconciliation with the Holy One of Israel.

And that last Jewish sacrifice, at the hour of the crucifixion, which ended the "first" and began the "second"; was there not something specially solemn about it? Was there not something peculiar about it as the last? Like the last cedar of Lebanon, the last olive of Palestine, the last pillar of a falling temple that has stood for ages, the last representative of an ancient race, it could not but have something sacred, something noble about it.

An unbelieving Jew, worshipping in the temple, at the time would see nothing remarkable about it, save the unaccountable darkness which had for three hours covered Jerusalem, and the fearful earthquake, and the mysterious rending of the veil, the tidings of which would immediately spread both in the temple and the city. What can all this mean, he might say; but he knew not what they meant; nor that this was the last sacrifice, according to the purpose of the God of Israel. Not connecting the first with the second, nor the earthly with the heavenly, he would soon forget the darkness, and the earthquake, and the torn veil, coming next morning at nine o'clock to assist in the celebration of the morning-sacrifice. For the great break in the sacrifices was an invisible thing to him. To heaven it was visible, to angels it was visible, to faith it was visible; but not to unbelief. And unbelief would go on from day to day doting on the old sacrifice and admiring the old altar; till the Roman torch set fire to the goodly cedar of the holy places, and the Roman battle-axe shivered the altar in pieces, and brought to the ground porch, and tower, and wall,- -gate and bar, in one irrecoverable ruin; not one stone left upon another.

But how would a believing Jew view this last sacrifice? With mingled feelings in many ways; for as yet his eyes were but half opened; and though he might in a measure understand the first, he could not fully see the second, nor the first in connection with the second. It would still be to him sacred and venerable; though now he saw it, like the picture of a dissolving view, passing away and being replaced by another. Holy histories of his nation and precious recollections of his own experience would come up into view. From that sacrifice he had learned the way of forgiveness, perhaps from childhood. Often had the sight of it poured in happy thoughts and told him of the love of a redeeming God. Often had he stood at that altar with his little ones, and taught them from it the way of salvation through blood. Often had he seen the fire blazing and the smoke ascending, and the blood flowing, and he had mused over all these in connection with the first promise of Messiah's bruised heel, and the later prophecies of His pouring out His soul unto death. But now he was startled. That darkness, that earthquake, that rent veil; and in connection with all this, the scene in Golgotha now going on, seemed to say that sacrifice has done its work and must pass away. That has come at last which he had been long looking for; the better Lamb, the richer blood, the more perfect sacrifice. Now he sees the full meaning of the burnt-offering; now his faith lays its hand on the head of the true sacrifice; now he knows what John meant when he said, "Behold the Lamb of God"; and he can say with Simeon, "Lord, now lettest Thou thy servant depart in peace; for mine eyes have seen Thy salvation."

And with what thoughts must the Son of God have seen from the cross the smoke of that last burnt- offering ascending? For it was at the ninth hour, our three o'clock, when the evening lamb was laid on the altar, that Jesus "cried with a loud voice, Eloi, Eloi, lama sabachthani?" Yes, when the Son of God, the true Sin-bearer, was uttering these words, Israel's last sacrifice was offered. It is finished, was the voice from the altar; it is finished was the voice from the cross. Now the last type is done; and Jesus sees it (for the altar-smoke would be quite visible from Golgotha); Israel's long lesson of ages has been taught; the type and Antitype have been brought face to face. How often had Jesus seen the morning and evening lamb offered up; and in gazing on it realised his own sin-bearing work. Now he sees all accomplished; sin borne, peace made, God propitiated; and in testimony of this the last burnt-sacrifice offered up. All is done. He sees of the travail of His soul and is satisfied. He can now tell Jew and Gentile that atonement has been made by the better blood. Life has been given for life; a divine life for a human. He can say, Look no longer on yon altar; its work is done. Look to me, of whom it spoke during so many ages; look unto me and be ye saved, all the ends of the earth.

And how does the Father view that last sacrifice? For four thousand years it had been the witness to the sin-bearing work of the coming Messiah. The Father had set it there to bear testimony to the propitiation of His Son. It said to Israel, and it said to the world before the days of Israel, The seed of the woman is to be man's deliverer. He is coming! He is coming to bear sin; to be wounded for our transgressions and bruised for our iniquities; to take the chastisement of our peace upon Him, and to heal us by His stripes. For ages that was the voice that came from the altar. It was the Father's voice foretelling the advent of His beloved Son. And now that voice from the altar is to die away. The testimony is to cease; for He to whom it was given is come. The ages of delay are over; the day of expectation has come to an end. The purpose of Jehovah is now consummated. The Father now delights in the accomplishment of His eternal design. Now grace and righteousness are one. So long as one burnt-offering remained unpresented, there was something awanting; something unfinished. But now the last of the long series has arrived. The type is perfected, the last stone has been laid; the last touch has been given to the picture; the last stroke of the chisel has fallen upon the statue. The imperfect has ended in the perfect, the unreal in the real; the first has become the last and the last first. Now divine love can take its unimpeded way; no drag, no uncertainty, no imperfection now. Grace and righteousness have become one. The Father's testimony to the finished work of His Son now goes forth to the ends of the earth. That last sacrifice on Israel's altar was the signal for the forthgoing of the world- wide message of pardon,--righteous pardon,--to the guiltiest, the saddest and the neediest of the sons of men.

And how is this last sacrifice viewed by the Church of God? Not with regret, nor with disappointment at the thought that there is no such altar now; but with rejoicing that the work has been at length consummated, and that there is no necessity for the repetition of the sacrifice. Whilst to a believing Jew there was satisfaction in each recurring sacrifice day by day, there could not but be a feeling of uneasiness at that very repetition. If the sacrifice is sufficient, why repeat it? Or will the multiplication of imperfections produce perfection? If insufficient, what is there to look to for the pacification of the conscience? But the termination of the series was an unspeakable relief. It was the winding up of a work which had been going on for four thousand years. Now, then, God is satisfied. Now there is the certainty of remission. Now the conscience is purged. Now the soul is at rest. And thus that last burnt-offering gave to the Church the assurance that the reconciliation was accomplished. No more offering for sin! No more blood! the foundation is now secure. On it she stands, in it she rejoices. The "good conscience" is now secured. Fear and shame in drawing near to God are at an end for ever. There is nothing but boldness now; for by one offering He hath perfected for ever them that are sanctified. Not by the blood of goats and calves, but by His own blood, He hath entered in once into the holy place, having obtained eternal redemption for us. By this blood He hath reconciled us to Himself. By this blood He daily cements the reconciliation, and keeps our souls in peace. By this blood He washes off the ever-recurring sins that would come between us and God, purging our consciences from dead works to serve the living God (Heb 9:12,13).

Round the old altar on Moriah one nation gathered, for the worship of Jehovah, during a few earthly ages; but round the new altar is gathered the great multitude that no man can number, out of every nation and people; for we have an altar, whereof they have no right to eat who serve the tabernacle. The first has been taken away, but the second has been set up, to stand for ever. Here we worship now; here shall be the eternal worship; the Lamb slain is the centre of worship for the universe of God, whether on earth, or in heaven, or throughout the wide regions which the creating Word has filled with suns and stars. On this divine altar shall all creaturehood lay its everlasting praise. From this altar shall ascend the never-ending son. This altar shall be the great centre of unity between the multitudinous parts or units of universal being. Here heaven and earth shall meet; here redeemed men and angels shall hold fellowship; here the principalities and powers in heavenly places shall learn the wisdom of God; here shall be found the stability, not of manhood only, but of creaturehood as well, the divine security against a second fall, against any future failure of creation, against any future curse, against the possibility of evil or weakness or decay. He has taken away the first, but He has established the second; and with that He has linked the establishment of all that is good and holy and blessed in His universe for evermore.

From this "second" also there goes forth the message of reconciliation; the announcement that peace has been made through the blood of the cross; the entreaty on the part of God, that each distant one would draw near, each wanderer re-enter his Father's house. To every one that is afar off, this great propitiation speaks, and says, RETURN! It bids you welcome, with all your worthlessness and unfitness, pointing to the ever-open door, and assuring you of reception, and pardon, and free love, without delay, without condition, and without upbraiding. From this centre the good news of God's free love to the unrighteous are going forth. In the simple reception of these by the sinner there is everlasting life; but in the non-reception of them there is eternal death; for that blood condemns as well as justifies. It speaks peace, but it speak trouble and anguish. It contains life, but it also contains death. It introduces into heaven, but it casts down to hell. He who receives it is washed, and sanctified, and justified; he who rejects it is undone,--doomed to bear his own guilt, without reprieve, for ever. For you, or against you, through eternity that blood must be.

There has been a first, there is a second, but there shall be no third! The first could not suffice, either for salvation or for destruction; it did not save those who used it, nor did it ruin those who used it not, or who used it amiss. The second sufficed for both. It is able to save and to destroy, to forgive and to condemn. No third is needed, no third is possible. The second is established for ever. It is eternal. It is an everlasting sacrifice. It is an eternal ransom, an eternal redemption, an eternal salvation, an everlasting covenant, and an everlasting gospel. Its accompaniments and issues are everlasting life, everlasting habitations, everlasting consolation, an everlasting kingdom, an eternal inheritance, an eternal weight of glory, a house not made with hands, eternal in the heavens. Yes; this second is established, and shall stand for ever. He who accepts it becomes, like it, established, and shall stand for ever; for it has the power of imparting its stability to every one who receives God's testimony concerning it. This is "the living stone, disallowed indeed of men, but chosen of God, and precious; to which coming we, as living stones, are built up a spiritual house, an holy priesthood, to offer up spiritual sacrifices acceptable to God by Jesus Christ" (1 Peter 2:4,5).

There shall be no third! This is the security and the joy of all who receive it. He who has taken away the first has established the second. Heaven and earth may pass away, but it must remain; and with it remains our reconciliation, our sonship, our royalty, and our eternal weight of glory. Were it possible that this second altar could be overthrown, or crumble down through age; this second blood, and second covenant, and second priesthood become inefficacious or obsolete, then should our future be shaded with uncertainty. But all these being divine are eternal; and in their eternity is wrapt up that of every one who is now by faith partakers of them; in their eternity is wrapt up that of the inheritance, the city, and the kingdom, which become the possession of every one whom the blood has washed and reconciled.

For the cross is never old. The wood, and nails, and inscription have indeed perished long ago; but the cross in which Paul gloried stands for ever. That cross is the axle of the universe, and cannot snap asunder. That cross is the foundation on which the universe rests, and cannot give way. The cross of Golgotha is, in this sense, everlasting; and each one who glories in it becomes partaker of its immortality. In itself blood is the symbol of death; in connection with the cross of Christ, it is the emblem and the pledge of life. It is by blood that all that is feeble, and corruptible, and unclean is purged out of creature-hood. It is by blood that this race of ours is preserved against the possibility of a second fall, and this earth against the contingency of a second curse. It is by blood that the Church of God has won her victory, and been made without spot, or wrinkle, or any such thing. It is the blood that has given such resplendent glory to the New Jerusalem, and made its light so pure, for "THE LAMB is the light thereof."

And yet is it not on this very blood that the spirit of the age is pouring its contempt, as if it were the great disfiguration of Christianity, requiring to be explained and spiritualised, before it can be admitted to have any connection with a divine religion? Is it not against this blood that the tide of modern progress is advancing, to wash out every trace and stain of it? It is against the blood that unbelief is now specially declaring war, little supposing, in its blindness, what would be the consequences of success in this warfare. Take away that blood, and the security of the universe is gone. Take away the blood, and the gate of the glorious city closes against the sinner; nay, that city itself, with all its beauty, and purity, and splendour, passes away like a vision of the night, each stone of it vanishing into nothingness, and its light becoming darkness.

Chapter 7

Messiah Within the Veil

We spoke of Messiah longing for the time when the veil should be rent, and when, through Himself, there should be unobstructed access to the innermost shrine of God. "How am I straitened till it be accomplished." We spoke also of His dreading this rending, this death,--so that "with strong crying and tears He prayed to Him who was able to save Him from death" (Heb 5:7).

Let us now see Him looking beyond the veil, surveying the glory, and anticipating His own entrance into it, as our forerunner, the first fruits of them that slept, the first-begotten of the dead. "For the joy set before Him He endured the cross, despising the shame, and is now set down at the right hand of God" (Heb 12:2). That to which He looked forward was not so much the rending of the veil, as the result of that rending,--both for Himself and for His Church, His body, the redeemed from among men.

The veil was rent; rent "once for all"; rent for ever. Yet there was a sense in which it was to be restored, though after another fashion than before. Messiah could not be "holden" by death, because He was the Holy One, who could not see corruption. Death must be annulled. The broken body must be made whole; resurrection must come forth out of death; and that resurrection was to be life, and glory, and blessedness. Through the rent veil of His own flesh, He was (if we may so use the figure) to enter into "glory and honour, and immortality." Thus He speaks in the sixteenth Psalm:-- "Therefore my heart is glad, Yea, my glory rejoiceth: My flesh also shall rest in hope. For thou wilt not leave my soul in hell; Neither wilt thou suffer thine Holy One to see corruption. Thou wilt show me the path of life: In thy presence is fulness of joy; At thy right hand are pleasures for evermore." Let us dwell upon these verses in connection with Messiah's entrance within the veil.

The speaker in this Psalm is undoubtedly Christ. This we learn from Peter's sermon at Jerusalem (Acts 2:25). He is speaking to the

Father, as His Father and our Father. He speaks as the lowly, depend-ent son of man; as one who needed help and looked to the Father for it; as one who trusted in the Lord and walked by faith, not by sight; as one who realised the Father's love, anticipated the joy set before Him, and had respect to the recompense of the reward.

He speaks, moreover, as one who saw death before Him,-- "Thou wilt not leave my soul in hell"; and looking into the dark grave, on the edge of which He was standing, just about to plunge into it, He casts His eye upwards and pleads, with strong crying and tears, for resurrection, and joy, and glory,-- "Thou wilt show me the path of life." For the words of the Psalm are the united utterances of confi-dence, expectation, and prayer; not unlike those of Paul, "I am now ready to be offered, and the time of my departure is at hand; hence-forth there is laid up for me a crown of righteousness."

He speaks too as one who was bearing our curse; as one who was made sin for us; and to whom everything connected with sin and its penalty was infinitely terrible; not the less terrible, but the more, because the sin and the penalty were not His own, but ours. The death which now confronted Him was one of the ingredients of the fearful cup, against which He prayed in Gethsemane, "Let this cup pass from me"; for we read that, "in the days of His flesh He made supplication, with strong crying and tears, unto Him that was able to save Him from death." In this Psalm, indeed, we do not hear these strong cryings and tears, which the valley of the Kedron then heard. All is calm; the bit-terness of death is past; the power of the king of terrors seems broken; the gloom of the grave is lost in the anticipated brightness of the resur-rection light and glory. But still the scene is similar; though in the Psalm the light predominates over the darkness, and there is not the agony, nor the bloody sweat, nor the exceeding sorrow. It is our Surety looking the king of terrors in the face; contemplating the shadows of the three days and nights in the heat of the earth; surveying Joseph's tomb, and while accepting that as His prison-house for a season, an-ticipating the deliverance by the Father's power, and rejoicing in the prospect of the everlasting gladness.

The first thing that occupies His thoughts is resurrection. The path of death is before Him; and He asks that He may know the path of life;--the way out of the tomb as well as the way into it. Death is to Him an enemy; an enemy from which as the Prince of life His holy soul would recoil even more than we. The grave is to Him a prison-house, gloomy as Jeremiah's low dungeon or Joseph's pit, not the less gloomy because He approaches it as a conqueror, as bringing life and immortality to light, as the resurrection and the life. Into that prison-house He must descend; for though rich He has stooped to be poor; and this is the extremity of his poverty, the lowest depth of His low estate,--even the surrender of that, for which even the richest on earth will part with everything,--life itself. But out of that dungeon He cries to be brought; and for this rescue He puts Himself entirely into the Father's hands, "Thou wilt show me the path of life."

Very blessed and glorious did resurrection seem in the eyes of the Prince of life, of Him who is the resurrection and the life. Infinitely hateful did death and the grave appear to Him who was the Conqueror of death, the Spoiler of the grave. He had undertaken to die, for as the second Adam He came to undergo the penalty of the first, "dust thou art and unto dust shalt thou return"; yet not the less bitter was the cup, not the less gloomy was the valley of the shadow of death; not the less welcome was the thought of resurrection.

The next thing which fills His thoughts is the presence of God,--that glorious presence which He had left when He "came down from heaven." His thoughts are of the Father's face, the Father's house, the Father's presence. Earth to Him was so different from heaven. He had not yet come to the "Why hast Thou forsaken me?" but He felt the dif-ference between this earth and the heaven He had quitted. There was no such "presence" here. All was sin, evil, hatred, darkness; the pres-ence of evil men and mocking devils; not the presence of God. God seemed far away. This world seemed empty and dreary. He called to mind the home, and the love, and the holiness He had left; and He longed for a return to these. "Thy presence!" What a meaning in these words, coming from the lips of the lonely Son of God in His desola-tion and friendlessness and exile here. "Thy presence!" How full of recollection would they be to Him as He uttered them; and how in-tensely would that recollection stimulate the anticipation and the hope!

Of this same Messiah, the speaker in the psalm, we read after-wards, "In the beginning was the Word, and the Word was with God, and the Word was God; the same was in the beginning with God" (John 1:1); and elsewhere He speaks thus of Himself: "Jehovah pos-sessed me in the beginning of His way, before His works of old; I was set up from everlasting, from the beginning, or ever the earth was...I was by Him, as one brought up with Him, and I was daily His delight, rejoicing always before Him" (Prov 8:22,30); and again, He, in the days of His flesh, thus prayed: "O Father, glorify Thou me with Thine own self, with the glory which I had with Thee before the world was" (John 17:5). Thus we see that the "presence" or "face" of God had been His special and eternal portion. His past eternity was associated entirely with this glorious presence. No wonder then that in the day of His deepest weakness,--when the last enemy confronted Him with his hideous presence, He should recall the Father's presence; anticipating the day of restoration to that presence, and repossession of the glory which He had before the world was.

"Thy presence," said the only-begotten of the Father looking up into the Father's face! He speaks as the sin-bearer, on whom the chastisement of our sins was laid, and between whom and heaven these sins had drawn a veil; He speaks as an exile, far from home, weary, troubled, exceeding sorrowful even unto death; He speaks as a Son feeling the bitterness of separation from His Father's presence, and of distance from His Father's house; He speaks as one longing for home and kindred, and the unimpeded outflowings of paternal love. "Thy presence," says the Man of sorrows looking round on an evil world;-- oh, that I were there! "Thy presence," says the forsaken Son of man, for "lover and friend hast Thou put far from me, and mine acquaintance into darkness";--oh, that I were there! "Thy presence," not this waste howling wilderness, this region of pain, and disease, and sin, and death, and tombs. "Thy presence," not these temptations, these devils, these enemies, these false friends; not this blasphemy, this reproach, this scorn, this betrayal, this denial, this buffeting, this scourging, this spitting, this mockery! "Thy presence,"--oh, that I were there; nevertheless, not my will but Thine be done.

Only through death can He reach life, for He is burdened with our sin and our death; and death is to Him the path of life. He must go through the veil to enter into the presence of God. Only through the grave,--the stronghold of death, and of him who has the power of death,--can He ascend into the presence of God; and therefore, when about to enter the dark valley, He commits Himself to the Father's guidance, to the keeping of Him who said, "Behold my servant whom I uphold," the keeping of which He himself, by the mouth of David, had spoken: "Yea, though I walk through the valley of the shadow of death, I will fear no evil, for Thou art with me, Thy rod and Thy staff they comfort me." Bethlehem, Egypt, Nazareth, Capernaum, Gethsemane, Golgotha,--these were all but stages in His way up to "the presence"--the presence of the Father; and it is when approaching the last of these, with the consciousness of His nearness to that presence, only one more dark passage to wind through, that He gives utterance to this psalm,--His psalm in prospect of resurrection and glory,-- "I have set the Lord always before me; because He is at my right hand, I shall not be moved: therefore my heart is glad and my glory rejoiceth; my flesh also shall rest in hope; for Thou wilt not leave my soul in hell, neither wilt Thou suffer Thine holy One to see corruption; Thou wilt show me the path of life: in Thy presence is fulness of joy; at Thy right hand there are pleasures for evermore."

Connected with this "presence," this glory within the veil, he speaks of "fulness of joy." On earth, in the day of His banishment here, He found want, not fulness. He was poor and needy; no house, no table, no chamber, no pillow of His own. His was the extremity of human poverty; though rich He had become poor; he was hungry, thirsty, weary, with no place to lay His head. Though He knew no sin, He tasted the sinner's portion of want and sorrow. He was in the far country, the land of the mighty famine; and looking upwards to the happy heaven which He had left, He could say, "How many servants in my Father's house have bread and to spare, and I perish with hunger." Drinking also of the sinner's deep cup of wrath, He was the man of sorrows and acquainted with grief. It was as such that He looked up so often as we find Him in the Gospels doing, and as we find Him in this Psalm, with wistful eye reminding Himself of the joy He had left, and anticipating the augmented joy that was so soon to be His when, having traversed this vale of tears, and passed through the gates of death, He was to re-ascend to His Father, and re-enter the courts of glory and joy. "Fulness of joy" is His prospect; fulness of joy in the presence of God. Concerning this going to the Father He spoke to His disciples; and then added, "These things have I spoken unto you that my joy might remain in you, and that your joy might be full." It is of this same full joy that He speaks in our psalm; a joy which was to be the fulness of all joy; a joy which was to be His recompense for the earthly sorrow of His sin-bearing life and death; a joy which He was to share with His redeemed, and on which they too should enter, when they, like Him, had triumphed over death, and been caught up into the clouds to meet Him in the air; a joy which would be to them, in that wondrous day, infinitely more than a compensation for earthly tribulation; even as one of themselves has written, "Our present light affliction, which is but for a moment, worketh for us a far more eceeding and eternal weight of glory."

This was "the joy set before Him," because of which He endured the cross; and here He calls it FULNESS OF JOY. That which He calls fulness must be so; for He knows what joy is, and what its fulness is; just as He knew what sorrow was and its fulness. The amount of joy sufficient to fill a soul like His must be infinite; it must be joy unspeakable and full of glory. The amount of joy reckoned by the Father sufficient as the reward of the sorrow of such a Son, must be infinite indeed. What then must that be which Messiah reckons the fulness of joy. What a day was that for Him when, death and sorrow ended, He entered on life and gladness! And what a day will that be, yet in store for Him and for His saints, when we, as His joint-heirs, shall enter on all that life and gladness; the day of His glorious coming, when that shall be fulfilled which is written, "Come forth, O ye daughters of Jerusalem, and behold King Solomon with the crown wherewith his mother crowned him, in the day of his espousals, and in the day of the gladness of his heart."

Besides the "presence" or "face" of God within the veil, Messiah sees the right hand; the place of honour and power and favour,--the right hand of the throne of the majesty in the heavens; and at that right hand there are pleasures for evermore; eternal enjoyments, such as eye hath not seen, nor ear heard. For all the things on which Messiah's soul rests are everlasting; the life, the fulness, the joy, the presence, the pleasures,--all eternal! No wonder, then, that He who knows what eternity is,--an eternity of glory and gladness,--should feel that "the sufferings of this present time are not worthy to be compared with the glory that shall be revealed"; and should, when going up to the cross, and down into the grave, say with calm but happy confidence, "Thou wilt show me the path of life, in Thy presence is fulness of joy, at Thy right hand are pleasures for evermore." Most mysterious are such words as these from the lips of Him who is the resurrection and the life; and yet it is just because they come from Him,--from this Prince of Life,--that they are so assuring, so comforting to us. His oneness with us, and our oneness with Him, account for all the mystery. His oneness with us, as our substitute and sinbearer, the endurer of our curse and cross and death, accounts for all that is mysterious in this Psalm. Our oneness with Him clears up all that is wonderful in such words as "I am the resurrection and the life, he that believeth on me, though he were dead, yet shall he live." Blessed, thrice-blessed oneness,--mutual oneness; He one with us, we one with Him, in life, in death, in burial, in resurrection, and in glory. Now we can take up His words as truly meant for us, "Thou wilt show us the path of life"; for in believing God's testimony to the Messiahship of Jesus of Nazareth, we have become one with Him!

In all this we have,

1. Messiah's estimate of death. He abhors it. It is His enemy as well as ours. He came to conquer it, to destroy it for ever. He conquers

it by being conquered by it; He slays it by allowing Himself to be slain by it. He crucifies it, kills it, buries it for ever. Death is swallowed up in victory. "O death," He says, "I will be thy plague; O grave, I will be thy destruction."

2. Messiah's estimate of resurrection. He longs for it; both on His own account and His people's. It is the consummation of that which He calls life. It is the second life, more glorious than the first; the opposite extreme of being to that which is called "the second death." The Son of God came into the world as the Prince of Life; He came not merely that He might die, but that He might live; and that all who identify themselves with Him by the acceptance of the divine testimony concerning His life and death and resurrection, might not only have life, but might have it more abundantly. Resurrection is our hope, even as it was His; the first, the better resurrection; and as we toil onwards in our pilgrimage, burdened with the mortality of this vile body, and seeing death on every side of us, we take up Messiah's words of hope and gladness, "Thou wilt show me the path of life."

3. Messiah's estimate of joy. He recognises it as a thing greatly to be desired, not despised; as the true and healthy, or, as men say, the "normal" condition of creaturehood. God Himself is the blessed one; and He formed His creatures to be sharers of His blessedness. Heaven is full of joy; and all its dwellers are vessels of gladness. Earth was not made for sorrow, but for joy; and, before long, that song shall be sung over the new creation, "Let the heavens rejoice, and let the earth be glad." For this day of joy Christ longed, anticipating it as the consummation of all that He had come to do. As the eternal Word which was with the Father, He knew what joy was; as the Man of sorrows, He knew what sorrow was. He was in the true condition and circumstances to take the proper estimate of joy. And here He tells us what that estimate was. He longed to be done with sorrow, which was as the shadow of hell; He "desired with desire" to enter into the joy set before Him, the joy of life, the joy of resurrection, the joy of God's presence and right hand for ever. Let our eye, like His, be fixed on that coming gladness,--that sunrise of eternity for which the Church is waiting and creation groans. That hope will cheer, will nerve, will liberate, will heal, will animate, will purify; will do miracles for us. As yet, the joy has not arrived. It doth not yet appear what we shall be. Not now; not here; not on this side of the grave! But the promise of its possession, and the assurance that when it does arrive, it will be great enough and long enough to make up for all trial and all delay, are sufficient to keep us ever looking, waiting, watching. Resurrection is coming, with all its

light and joy; and then comes the world's second dawn, and the Church's long-expected dayspring; the cessation of creation's groans, the times of the restitution of all things; the new heavens and the new earth wherein dwelleth righteousness.

4. Messiah's estimate of the Father's love. It is this love that is His portion; it is in this love that He abides and rejoices; for it is He who says, "Thy loving kindness is better than life." No one knew so well as He did the glorious truth, "God is love; and he that dwelleth in love dwelleth in God, and God in him." The Father's love! Here His soul found its resting-place, in the midst of human hatred and reproach. The Father's love! It was with this that He comforted Himself, and with this it was that He comforted His Church, saying, "As the Father hath loved me, so have I loved you"; "Thou hast loved them as thou hast loved me"; "Thou lovedst me before the foundation of the world"; "that the love wherewith Thou hast loved me may be in them, and I in them." Is that love to us what it was to Him? It was His rest, is it ours? It was into this hidden chamber, this holy of holies, that He retired, when the world's storms beat upon Him; is it in this that we take refuge in our evil days? It was sufficient for His infinitely capacious soul; it may well suffice for ours. Is, then, His estimate of the Father's love our estimate? Is this love our gladness? Is its sunshine the brightness of our daily life? And with simple confidence in it, like Messiah's, do we look into and look through the future, however dark, saying, "Thou wilt show me the path of life; in Thy presence is fulness of joy, and at Thy right hand are pleasures for evermore?"

On all that light, and joy, and fulness, and love, Messiah has now entered. For eighteen hundred years He has been in that presence, and at that right hand, which He longed for; and though yet greater things are in store for Him in the day of His promised advent, yet He has now for ages been done with sorrow and death, with reproach and hatred. He has entered on His rest; He has passed into life; His blessedness is now without a shadow. And is not this a thought full of joy to us? He whom we love is happy! No second Gethsemane nor Golgotha for Him. Whatever may befall us, whatever of tribulation we may have yet to pass through, He is blessed; it is all well with Him. He has trodden the path of life; He has entered into that presence which He longed for; He has sat down at that right hand where there are pleasures for evermore. Is this not a joyful thought to us here, even in the midst of our weakness and sorrow? And was it not to this He referred when He said, "If ye loved me, ye would rejoice, because I said I go unto the Father"? and was it not with forgetfulness of this that He reproached His disciples, "Now I go my way to Him that sent me, and none of you asketh me, whither goest Thou? but because I have said these things unto you, sorrow hath filled your heart."

Should we not rejoice in His joy? Should not the thought of His happiness be a continual source of consolation to us? Amid the dreariness of the desert, it was a cheering thought to Israel that there was such a region as Canaan, over which the barrenness of the waste howling wilderness had no power. Amid the griefs and cares of earth, it is a blessed thought to us that there is such a place as heaven, to which the storm reaches not, and where there has never been known, neither shall be, one cloud, one pain, one sin. So amid the troubles of our own troubled spirits, or the sorrows of those about us, it is a happy thought that there is one heart, once full of grief, that now grieves no more; one eye that often wept, which now weeps no more; and that this blessed One is none other than our beloved Lord,--once the Man of sorrows. He who loved us, He whom, not having seen, we love, is now for ever blessed; He has entered that presence where there is fulness of joy; He has taken His seat at that right hand, where there are pleasures for evermore.

Does not this comfort and gladden us? What He now is, and what we so soon shall be,--this gives vigour and consolation. It lifts us almost unconsciously into a calmer region, and gives us to breathe the very air of the kingdom. It purifies, too, and strengthens; it makes us forget the things which are behind, and reach forward to what lies before.

The prospect of resurrection and glory sustained the soul of our Surety here. This was the joy set before Him. Let us set it before ourselves, that we may not be moved. We have much to do both with the future and the past. In that future lies our inheritance, and we cannot but be seeking to pierce the veil that hides it. But in the past we find our resting-place. Christ has ascended on high, leading captivity captive; he has ascended to His Father and our Father, to His God and our God. The work is done. The blood is shed. The fire has consumed the sacrifice. It is finished! This is the testimony which we bring from God, in the belief of which we are saved. It needs no second sacrifice; no repetition of the great burnt-offering. That which saves the sinner is done. Another has done it all. Messiah has done it all; and our gospel is not a command to do, but simply to take what another has done. He who ceases from His own labours, and enters on these labours of another, has taken possession of all to which these labours entitled Him, who so performed them, even the Messiah of Israel, the Son of God, the Saviour of the world

Chapter 8

The Blood Within the Veil

The day of atonement brought the three courts of the tabernacle into one. On that day the high priest passed from the outmost to the innermost; implying that he had equally to do with all the holy places, and that they whom he represented had also to do with these.

He carried the incense from the golden altar into the holiest; and he carried the blood from the brazen altar into the same. It was one blood, one incense, one priest for all the three.

The blood, which was sprinkled on the mercy-seat, was from without. The sacrifice was not slain in the inner courts, but in the outer. It was blood from without that was carried in the priestly basin within the veil, sprinkling the veil, the floor, the ark, the mercy-seat, and the feet of the cherubim as they stood upon the golden covering. In being carried within, it lost none of its expiating virtue and value: nay, it seemed to acquire more virtue and more value as it lay upon the furniture of the holy of holies.

Its efficacy, when thus brought within the veil, was enhanced; and it did not the less speak to those without because itself was within. It had come from without, and its voice spoke to those who were without. It spoke but from one small point, yet it goes beyond the tabernacle, beyond Israel, beyond Palestine, to the men of every kindred and nation, and tongue and people. It contained a world-wide message, so that each one hearing of that atoning blood might at once say, Then God is summoning me back to Himself; He is saying to me, "be thou reconciled to me"; He is sending to me, from the altar and the mercy-seat, an invitation of mingled righteousness and grace.

This propitiation rests on substitution. In all these symbolical transactions we have one vast thought,--the transference of guilt from one to another, legally and judicially; the presentation of one death for another, as perfectly valid for all ends of justice, and quite as suitable before God as the judge, to meet every governmental claim as the direct infliction of the appointed penalty on the actual transgressor.

There are two things which the whole Levitical service assumes, and without which it is simple mockery of man, that Sin is reality, and that Substitution is righteousness.

1. Sin is a real thing. Men do not think so, even when with their lips they utter the word. It is but a shadow to them, a mere name, no more.

Sin is a sore evil. It is not felt to be so, yet it is not the less truly such. It is not hated, it is not shunned as an evil,--an evil whose greatness no one can measure or tell. When men speak of it they do so as painters speak of shade in a scene or picture; as rather a needful thing, nay, a thing of beauty in its own way. They have no due sense or estimate of it at all. It is not to them what it is to God. It is not by any means in their books what it is in the book of God.

Yet, right views of sin are the key to the Bible, the key to the history of the world, and the key to God's purposes concerning it. He who does not know what sin is cannot understand the Bible. It must be a dark and strange book to him. He cannot solve the difficulties of the world's history. All is perplexed and contradictory. He cannot enter into God's purposes respecting it either in curse or in blessing, either in condemnation or redemption. Sin is not misfortune, but guilt; not disease, but crime; not an evil, but the evil, the evil of evils, the root of all evils; terrible in itself as fraught with all that we call "moral evil," and terrible in its judicial effects as necessarily and inexorably bound up with irresistible and irreversible condemnation.

In spite of all the divine teaching, both in God's book and in the world's history, man refuses to believe that sin is what God has proclaimed it, and what its own development, in the annals of the ages, has shown that it really is.

The first and fundamental lesson of the Levitical service is the infinite evil of sin. Sacrifice is God's declaration of His estimate of SIN. Strike this thought out of it, and sacrifice is simple barbarism,--a coarse emblem of the vengeance of a Jupiter, or a Moloch, or a Baal upon helpless creaturehood.

2. Substitution is righteousness.--I do not argue this question; I merely indicate that scripture assumes this.

Often has the doctrine of substitution been evil spoken of as a slander against God's free love. It has been called a commercial transaction, a bargain inconsistent with true generosity, a money-payment of so much love for so much suffering. Philosophy, falsely so called, has frequently, by such representations, striven to write down a truth for which it could not find a niche in its speculations, and of which the philosopher himself had never felt His need. With any book less buoyant than the Bible to float it up, this doctrine must long before this have been submerged under the weight of ridicule, which the wisdom of this world has brought to bear upon it.

But it has been seen that the Bible and the truth of substitution cannot be sundered. They must sink or float together. The great philosophic puzzle with many, who were not prepared to cast off the Scriptures, was how to disentangle the two, so as to strike out the doctrine and yet preserve the old Book.

This difficulty has been felt all the more, because in the Bible itself there are no indications of any misgivings as to the doctrine, no explanations meant to smooth angularities and make the doctrine less philosophically objectionable. As if unconscious of the force of any such objection, it makes use of figures, once and again, which are directly taken from the commercial transactions of life. Even if what is branded as the mercantile theology could be proved untrue, it is certainly very like what we find in the Bible; nor can one help feeling that if the above theology be untrue, it is rather strange that the Bible should lay itself so open to the suspicion of favouring it. For, after all, the strongest statements and most obnoxious figures are those of that Book itself. Eliminate these and we are ready to hear how philosophy can argue. We do not say "explain them," we say "eliminate them"; for our difficulty lies in the simple existence of such passages. Why are they there, if substitution and transference be not true? They are stumbling-blocks and snares. Let these passages themselves bear the blame, if blame there is. It is idle to revile a doctrine, yet leave the figures, from which it is drawn, untouched and uncondemned.

Substitution may be philosophical or unphilosophical, defensible or indefensible; still it is imbedded in the Bible; specially in the sacrificial books and sacerdotal ordinances. Its writers may be credited or discredited; but no one can deny that substitution was an article of their creed, and that they meant to teach this doctrine if they meant anything at all. We might as well affirm that Moses did not mean to teach creation in Genesis, or Israel's deliverance in Exodus, as that he did not profess to promulgate Substitution in Leviticus. Substitution is in that book beyond all question; along with that book let it stand or fall.

There is then substitution revealed to us beyond mistake in Scripture; revealed in connection with Israel's worship, Israel's tabernacle, and Israel's Messiah. The special thing in that service, in that sanctuary, and in that Deliverer, with which substitution is connected, is THE BLOOD. Hence it is with blood that we find atonement, expiation, and propitiation connected. For the blood is the life; and it is the substitution of one life for another that accomplishes these results, and brings with it these blessings to the guilty.

Let me take two passages, one from the Old Testament, the other from the New, in illustration of what the blood is affirmed to be and to do. I give but a brief sketch of what I suppose they include; but it will suffice to show what Scripture teaches on the subject.

The first is Zechariah 9:11, "As for thee also, BY THE BLOOD OF THY COVENANT I have sent forth thy prisoners out of the pit wherein is no water." Blood here is declared to be the cause of deliverance,--the blood of the covenant; as if without this covenanted blood-shedding there could be no setting free of the prisoner. The blood goes in, the prisoner comes out. The blood touches his chain, and it falls off. The blood drops on the prison-bar, and the gate flies open. It is blood that does it all; blood whose virtue is recognised by God; blood whose effects and results are embraced in the everlasting covenant; the covenant of peace, the covenant of deliverance, the covenant of liberty, the covenant of life. But let us look more closely at the language of the prophet.

The words "as for thee also," or "thou also," are the very words of our Lord, when weeping over Jerusalem; "Even thou," thou, the guiltiest of the guilty, the most undeserving and unloveable of all. Thus our text starts with a declaration of the great love of God,-- Messiah's love to Israel,-- "Yea, He loved the people." "God is love," runs through this whole passage; and "where sin abounded grace did much more abound."

To this passage the apostle seems to refer in Hebrews 13:20, as to the bringing up Christ from the dead by the blood of the everlasting covenant. The prophet's words were fulfilled in Christ's resurrection, as Hosea's (11:1) were in his return from Egypt. (See also Psalm 18 and 40)

The words of Zechariah shall yet be fulfilled in Israel. The day of deliverance for the beloved nation is surely coming. She shall know the power of the covenant-blood to protect, to deliver, to save, to bless. It is not simply "blood" expiating sin in general, but "covenant-blood," linking that expiation specially to Israel, and Israel to it. It is passover-blood, bringing out of Egypt. Passing over this, however, let us take up the words in their widest sense. Let us see what the covenant-blood can do, not for Israel only, but for us.

The blood finds us "prisoners," captives, "lawful captives," exiles. It finds us righteously condemned, sold to our enemies, under wrath. Let us see what it does for us.

1. It removes the necessity for imprisonment. Such a necessity did exist. Law must take its course. Its claims must be satisfied. No leaving the prison till the uttermost farthing has been paid. The blood has made the satisfaction. It has met the claim. It has provided for the payment of the penalty. The necessity for the imprisonment no longer exists. The law consents.

2. It makes it right for God to deliver. Deliverance must be the work of righteousness, not of Almightiness alone. It was righteousness that sent the sinner to prison, and barred the door against all exit. It is righteousness that must bring him forth; and this righteousness is secured by the blood of the covenant. It is now as unrighteous to detain the captive, as before it would have been unrighteous to bring him forth.

3. It opens the prison-door. That door is locked, and barred, and guarded. No skill can open it, no force can unbar it, no money can bribe its guards. It cannot be opened by the earthquake, or the fire, or the lightning. Only righteousness can open it; and that prison-opening righteousness comes through the blood of the covenant; the great blood-shedding makes the prison-gates fly open; it rolls away the stone.

4. It makes it safe for the prisoner to come forth. For the avenger stands without, on the watch. He has a right to be there. He has a right to seize the prisoner, and to take vengeance. But the blood stays all this. The covenant-blood conducts the prisoner forth, and the sight of it bids the avenger flee. That avenger was the executioner of guilt, and the guilt is gone. The blood has removed that which gave him power. He sees the blood, and withdraws his hand.

5. It reconciles to God. It is the blood of propitiation, the blood of atonement. It makes up the variance between the sinner and God. It removes the ground of distance and dispeace. It brings nigh those that were afar off, by making distance no longer a righteous necessity, and nearness a thing of which the law approves, and in which God delights. It is reconciling blood.

6. It redeems. "Thou hast redeemed us to God by Thy blood." It is the ransom or purchase-money. It was necessary that the sinner, sold and imprisoned, should be bought back again at a price such as would satisfy law and justice. And the blood has been found to be ample

payment,--the very ransom needed by those whom death had made captive.

7. It cleanses. We are washed from our sins in this covenant-blood; our robes are washed white in the blood of the Lamb. All that sin had done this blood undoes. All its pollution this blood washes away. It is purifying blood; and, as such, it fits for worship, for drawing near to God.

8. It pacifies. It comes into contact with the sinner's conscience, and removes the sense of guilt,-- takes away the terror. The soul is at peace, and is kept in peace by this blood. "He has made peace by the blood of His cross."

Let these things suffice to show the power of the covenant-blood. Such it was, such it is, such it will be.

It is as efficacious as ever. It has lost none of its power. Age does not change it, nor repeated use weaken its efficacy. It can still do all it once did for the sinner. Its potency is divine.

It is as sufficient, as suitable, as free, as near as ever. He whose blood it is comes up to each of us, and presents it to us in all its fulness and power. Take it as it is presented, and all the benefits of this covenant-blood forthwith become yours; and though you may be the unworthiest of the unworthy, you are reckoned by God clean every whit; a forgiven sinner, a delivered prisoner, a saved man.

The second passage to which I would refer is Hebrews 10:19:-- "Having therefore, brethren, boldness to enter into the holiest (or literally 'the holies' 'or holy places') by the blood of Jesus; by a new and living way which He hath consecrated for us, through the veil, that is to say his flesh; and having an High Priest over the house of God, let us draw near with a true heart, in full assurance of faith, having our hearts sprinkled from an evil conscience, and our bodies washed with pure water."

As in the former passage, so in this, it is only a brief sketch that I can here give; not attempting to expound the words or illustrate the argument, but to bring out the emboldening of which the apostle speaks in connection with the blood. Deliverance by the blood was the idea of the former passage; boldness by the blood is the idea of this. The boldness comes to us from what that blood reveals to us of God, and of the way in which He has met the sinner and provided for his entrance into the sanctuary as a worshipper.

It is not so much doctrine that the apostle delivers to us in his Epistles, as "the fulness of Christ," that fulness as supplying the sinner's wants and as bringing him into that relationship to God, which

God's purpose of redemption designed, and which was needful for the sinner's blessedness.

God's full provision in Christ for us as sinners is continually brought before us; and we are invited to avail ourselves of it. The provision for the removal of wrath, for pardon, for reconciliation, for service, is fully detailed, that we may know the "manifold grace of God" and "the unsearchable riches of Christ." For instance:--

In the Epistle to the Romans we have the provision in Christ fitting us for work:--viz., that righteousness of God which delivers us from condemnation and sets us free to serve or work for Him who hath delivered us: and in the last chapter of that epistle we have the list of a noble band of apostolic workers.

In the Epistle to the Ephesians we have the provision for conflict:--viz, the being filled with the Spirit and His gifts, that we may wrestle against principalities and powers. The armour and weapons for the warfare are described in the concluding chapter.

In the Epistle to the Hebrews we have the provision for worship. For God is seeking worshippers, and He has made provision for making such. It is to worship that He calls us in this epistle; and He points to that which enables us to become acceptable worshippers:--to that which, so soon as it is understood and believed, turns the chief of sinners and the farthest off of prodigals into an acceptable and happy worshipper.

He assumes that "boldness" or "confidence" is essential to this: and this boldness has been provided. There is, 1. the open door of the sanctuary; 2. liberty to enter; 3. boldness in drawing near to God; 4. access to all the courts; for the expression is not simply "the holiest" but "the holy places"; as if we had the fullest right to every part of the sanctuary, the full range of the holy places.

This boldness is the opposite of dread, and darkness, and suspicion, and uncertainty. It is not merely the reversal of Adam's flying from God into the trees of the garden, but it is the entire removal of all sense of danger, or fear of unacceptableness,-- nay, it is the importation of childlike and unhesitating confidence, in virtue of which we go in without trembling and without blushing; for God's provision is so ample that in going into His courts and going up to His throne we are neither afraid nor ashamed. All that would have produced such feelings has been taken away. This boldness is effected,

1. By something without us. It is not anything within us,--our evidences, or experiences, or feelings; not even our regeneration, and

our being conscious of the Spirit's work in us. It is entirely by something without us,--the blood of Jesus.

2. By something in the heavens. It is into the heaven of heavens that we are to enter in worshipping God; and that which gives us boldness in entering there, must be something which has been presented there, as the apostle says,-- "the heavenly things themselves by better sacrifices than these." The blood was shed on earth, but presented in heaven; Christ entered in with His own blood.

3. By something about which there can be no mistake. The question as to the existence of the blood or its being presented in heaven, is settled once for all on the authority of God. We need not reason about it. God has told us that it has been done. As to our own feelings there may be many mistakes; but as to the presentation of the blood, there can be no doubt and no mistake. It is a certainty; and on that certainty we rest.

4. By something which shows that the ground of dread is removed. The dread arose from the thought, 1. I am guilty; 2. God must be my enemy; 3. I dare not come near him; 4. He must condemn me. The blood of Jesus meets these causes of terror, and shows the provision which God has made for the removal of them all. The sight of the blood dispels my terror and relieves my conscience, and says, Be of good cheer. For it shows the penalty paid by a substitute,--the full penalty; a divine life given in room of a human life, the wages of sin paid by the death of a divine substitute.

5. By something which God has accepted. God has accepted the blood! He raised Him whose blood it is; and this was acceptance. He set Him on His throne at His right hand. This is acceptance. He presents him as the Lamb slain. This is acceptance. He has testified to His acceptance of it. It is blood which God has accepted for that pardon and cleansing and reconciling that we preach; blood by which law is magnified and righteousness exalted.

6. By something which glorifies God. That blood- shedding glorifies Him. The sinner's admission and entrance glorifies Him,-- glorifies Him more than his exclusion and banishment and death. The blood by which God is thus glorified in receiving the sinner, must give boldness. I am going in to glorify God; and my going in will glorify Him, in consequence of that blood,--this cannot but embolden me.

7. By something which tells that God wants my worship. God came down seeking worshippers. He wants your worship,--this is His message. That tabernacle says He wants you as a worshipper. That laver, blood, incense, mercy-seat, all say He wants you as a worship-

per. He is in earnest in seeking you to worship Him. He wants you to come in and serve in His courts,- -as a priest!

We go in through the open gate, the rent veil: by the new and living way, the blood-dropped pavement. Personally we are sprinkled from an evil conscience; i.e., at the altar; our bodies are washed, i.e., at the laver. Thus there are such things as the following, resulting from all this.

1. Liberty of conscience. I mean liberty of conscience before God. A "good conscience" comes to us through the blood upon the mercy-seat. A conscience void of offence before men we may have in other ways, but only in this can all have a conscience void of offence before the Searcher of hearts. It is the blood which purges the conscience from dead works, as did the water mixed with the ashes of the red heifer cleanse the Israelite who had touched a dead body. By the blood the "true heart" comes.

2. Confident approach to God. Instead of flying from God, we turn to Him. Instead of trembling as we cross the threshold of His sanctuary, we lift up our heads like those who know that only here are they on secure ground,--like the flying manslayer entering the gate of the Refuge City. The blood removes the dread, and makes us feel safe even under the holy light of the glory. We are protected by the blood; we are comforted by the blood: for this blood casteth out all fear.

3. Happy intercourse. A sinner's fellowship with God must be carried on through the blood. That blood was meant to remove everything that would have hindered communion; or that would have kept God at a distance from the sinner, and the sinner at a distance from God. But it is not merely that we are brought nigh by the blood of Christ; we are brought nigh in the fulness of a tranquil spirit, which feels that it can now unbosom itself to God, in the certainty of confiding love. Fear has been supplanted by joy. The intercourse is the intercourse of trusting happy hearts, pouring out their love into each other; and the Spirit bears witness to the blood in this respect, by imparting the childlike frame, and teaching us to cry Abba Father.

4. Spiritual service. There seems nothing spiritual in the blood; and yet without the blood spiritual service is an impossibility. Abel's sacrifice seemed a more carnal thing than Cain's offering of the choicest fruits of Eden, yet it was in Abel's that God recognised the spirituality and the acceptable service. It is the blood which divests us of that externalism which cleaves to the service of the sinner,--which strips us of a hollow ritualism; which turns death into life, hollowness into substance, and unreality into truth. Spiritual service has ever been

connected with the blood-shedding of atonement, which by its appeal to the inner man, draws out the whole spiritual being in happy obedience and willing devoted service.

5. Holy worship. Holiness is not associated with darkness, or gorgeous rites, or glittering robes, or fragrant incense, or swelling music, or a magnificent temple, or an unnumbered multitude. All these may be unholy things, hateful to God. There may be the absence of all these, and yet there may be holy worship: the worship of holy lips; the worship of holy hands; the worship of holy knees; the worship of a holy soul. It is the blood that consecrates; whether it be man or place, whether it be voice or soul. That which is presented to God must have passed through the blood, else it is unholy, however imposing and splendid. If it has come through the blood, it is holy, however small and mean and poor. All worship is unclean save that which has been sanctified by the blood. All holy worship begins with the blood, and is carried on by means of the blood. We go within the rent veil to worship, not without blood. For it is the blood which sprinkled on the worshipper makes him first, and then his worship, acceptable. This is "entire consecration."

Chapter 9

God Seeking Worshippers

For ages before God sought a temple, He had been seeking worshippers. He could do without the former, but not without the latter.

His first sanctuary was but a tent; and three thousand years had elapsed before He said, Build me a house wherein I may dwell. Yet all this time He was seeking for worshippers amongst the sons of men. By man's sin God had lost the worship of earth, and He had set Himself to regain it.

1. He wants LOVE. Being the infinitely loveable God, He asks love from man--from every man; love according to His worth and beauty.

2. He claims OBEDIENCE. For His will is the fountainhead of all law; and He expects that this will of His should be in all things conformed to.

3. He expects SERVICE. The willing and living service of man's whole being is what He claims and desires,--the service of body, soul, and spirit.

4. He asks for WORSHIP. He does not stand in need of human praise or prayer; yet He asks for these, He delights in these, He wants the inner praise of the silent heart. He wants the uttered praise of the fervent lip and tongue. He desires the solitary praise of the closet; and still more the loud harmony of the great congregation; for "the Lord loveth the gates of Zion more than all the dwellings of Jacob," (Psa 87:2). True praise is a "speaking well of God", (1 Peter 1:3), speaking of Him in psalms and hymns and spiritual songs, according to His excellency. "Bless the Lord, O my soul" (Psa 103:1), "Blessed be the God and Father of our Lord Jesus Christ" (Eph 1:3).

It was of "worship" that the Lord spoke so much to the woman of Sychar. To Nicodemus He said nothing of this; nor indeed to any others. It was in regard to "worship" that the Samaritans had gone so far astray, therefore He speaks specially of this,--even to this poor profligate. He spoke to her of "the Father," and of "the worship of the

Father" (John 4:21); reminding her that God was a spirit and that "they who worship Him must worship Him in spirit and in truth." And then He adds these memorable words, "the Father seeketh such to worship Him."

It was of the difference between outward and inward religion, between the real and the unreal, between the acceptable and the unacceptable, that He spoke to the woman. Samaria and Jerusalem, Gerizzim and Moriah, these were but external things. There was no religious virtue connected with them; God is not the God of the outward, but of the inward; not the God of places, but of living creatures; not the God of cities and mountains, but the God of hearts and souls. No rites, however numerous or gorgeous or beautiful, can be a substitute for the life and the spirit. The question is not intellectual, or aesthetic, or pictorial, but spiritual; not as to what gratifies our eye or ear, our sense of the great or the tasteful, but what is acceptable to God and according to His instructions.

Where am I to worship God? man asks; but he answers it in his own way; as all false religions, and indeed some true ones, have done. On certain sacred spots, he says, where some man of God has lived, where some martyr's blood has been shed, where the footsteps of good men are recorded to have been, which have been consecrated by certain priestly rites,--there and there only must men worship God. God's answer to the question, Where am I to worship God? is, EVERYWHERE: on sea and land, vale or hill, desert or garden, city or village or moor,--anywhere and everywhere. For certain purposes God set apart Sinai for a season, and then Moriah; but not to the exclusion of other places. And even these consecrations are at an end. Sinai is but the old red granite hill,--no more,--where now no man worships. Moriah is but the old limestone platform, now desecrated by false worship. "Woman, believe me, the hour cometh, when ye shall neither in this mountain, nor yet at Jerusalem, worship the Father" (John 4:21).

When am I to worship God? man asks; but he answers it in his own way also. Only at certain times, he says,--certain hours, and certain days, fixed and arranged by priestly authority, or ecclesiastical law, or traditional rule. God's answer is, "at all times and seasons": pray without ceasing. The naming of certain hours and days is necessary for the gathering together of the worshippers; but worship is to be perpetual, without restriction of times. All hours are holy; all days are holy, in so far as worship is concerned; only one day having been specially appointed of God, and that not for restriction but for order.

How am I to worship God? man asks; and he has answered it also in his own way. In the gorgeous temple, in the pillared cathedral, with incense, and vestments, and forms, and ceremonies, and processions, and postures, he says.[14] But these performances are the will-worship of self-righteousness, not the obedient service of men worshipping God in ways of His own ordination. Man cannot teach man how to worship God. When he tries it he utterly fails. He distorts worship; he misrepresents God, and he indulges his own sensuous or self-righteous tastes. His "dim religious light" is but a reflection of his own gloomy spirit, and an ignorant misrepresentation of Him "who is light, and in whom is no darkness at all." God's answer to man's question is given in the Lord's words, "they that worship Him must worship Him in spirit and in truth." The vestments may or may not be comely; that matters not. The music may or may not be fine: the knees may or may not be bent; the hands may or may not be clasped; the place of worship may or may not be a cathedral, or a consecrated fabric. These are immaterial things; adjuncts of religion, not its essence. The true worship is that of the inner man; and all things else are of little moment. As it is with love so it is with worship. The heart is everything. God can do without the bended knee, but not without the broken heart.

It is of the Father that Christ is here speaking;--of Him whose name is not only God but Father,[15] the God and Father of our Lord Jesus Christ. As the fountainhead of all being in heaven and in earth, the paternal Creator, the Father of spirits, the great Father-spirit, the God of the spirits of all flesh, whom the heaven of heavens cannot contain, yet who visiteth earth in His fatherly love,--as such He is here spoken of by our Lord. He is a spirit, yet He is no vague or cold abstraction, no mere assemblage of what we call attributes, but full of life and love; with the heart of a Father, with the pity and power and care of a Father, and also with all a Father's resources and rights. Though we have broken off from that Father and gone into the far country, that does not change His paternal nature, though it alters our relationship to Him and the treatment we are to receive at His hands. He made the fatherly heart of man, and He did so after the likeness of His own. That fatherly heart yearns over His wandered family; "His tender mercies are over all His works."

It is as Father that he is seeking worshippers, and seeking them here on earth among the fallen sons of men.

He seeketh! That word means more than it seems. He is in search of something; of something which He has lost; of something which He counts precious; of something which He cannot afford to lose. Great as He is, there are many things which He cannot think of letting go. His very greatness makes Him needy for it makes Him understand the value, not only of every soul which He has formed, but of every atom of dust which He has created. When He misses any part of His creation He goes or sends in search of it; He will not part with it. Men of common souls, when they lose anything, are apt to say, Let it go, I can do without it. Men of great minds, when they lose anything, say, I must have it back again, I cannot afford to lose it. Much more is this true of the infinite Jehovah. It is His greatness that makes Him so susceptible of loss. Others may overlook the lost thing. He cannot. He must go in quest of it.

It is the same kind of seeking and searching as the prophet Ezekiel, speaking in the name of Jehovah, declares,-- "I will search and seek," (34:11); and to which our Lord so often refers, when He represents Himself as "seeking the lost" (Luke 19:10); it may be the lost sheep, or the lost piece of silver, or the lost son.

We must not dilute these expressions, and say that they simply imply that God is willing to have us back again if we will come; that He is willing to take us as worshippers if we will come. All that comes very far short of the meaning. And though we may say, what can the infinite Jehovah be in want of; what can He need, to whom belongs not only the heaven of heavens but the whole universe;--still we must see how anxious He is to show us His unutterable earnestness in seeking and in searching.

Such is the attitude of God! He bends down from His eternal throne to seek; as if the want of something here on earth, on this old sinful earth, would be a grievous and irreparable loss. What value does He attach to us and to our worship!

Yes, the Father seeketh worshippers! He is in search of many things of which sin has robbed Him; affection, homage, allegiance, reverence, obedience; but worship,--the worship of man, and of man's earth, He is specially seeking and claiming. He so created this world, that from it there should arise, without ceasing, wide as the universal air, that fragrance of holy worship, from the creatures which He had made and placed upon its surface. The command is not merely, "Thou shalt love the Lord thy God with all thy heart," but "thou shalt worship the Lord thy God and Him only shalt thou serve." Over this broken command He mourns; "it grieves Him at His heart"; and He seeks to have it restored in man. He loves worship from human hearts and lips, and He will not be satisfied without it. It might seem a small thing to lose the worship of a creature's heart, here on this low and evil earth.

Can He not let it go? It will only be the worse for the creature, not for Him, who has the worship of heaven, and of ten thousand times ten thousand angels. No; He cannot lose that worship. It is precious to Him. He must have it back.

O man, God speaks to you and says, "Worship me." He comes up to each sinner upon earth and says, "Worship me." If He does so, He must care for you and He must care for your worship. It is not a matter of indifference to Him whether you worship Him or not. It concerns Him, and it concerns you. Perhaps the thought comes up within you, what does God care for my worship? I may praise, or I may not, what does He care? I may sing, or I may blaspheme, what does it matter to Him? He cares much. It concerns Him deeply. He is thoroughly in earnest when He asks you to worship Him. He wants these lips of yours, that tongue of yours, that heart of yours. He wants them all for Himself. Will you give Him what He wants?

You say He has enough of praise in heaven, what can he want on earth? He has angels in myriads to praise Him, does He really desire my voice? Will He be grieved if I refuse it? Yes, He desires your voice, and He will be grieved if you withhold it. He has many a nobler tongue than yours, but still He wants yours. He has many a sweeter voice than yours, still He is bent on having that poor sinful voice. Oh come and worship me, He says.

This answers the question so often put by the inquiring, What warrant have I for coming to God. God wants you. Is not that enough? What more would you have? He wants you to draw near. He has no pleasure in your distance. He wants you to praise Him, to worship Him. He is seeking your worship. Do you mean to ask, What warrant have I for worshipping God? Rather should you ask, What warrant have I for refusing to worship Him? Is it possible that you can think yourself at liberty not to worship Him; nay, think that you are not under any obligation to worship Him, until you can ascertain your election, or feel within you some special change which you can consider God's call to worship Him?

His search for worshippers is a world-wide one. It goes over the whole earth; and His call on men to worship is equally universal. He made man to worship and to love; can He ever forego such claims, or can man ever be in a position in which that claim ceases, or that obligation is cancelled? Can his sinfulness or unworthiness exempt him from the duty, or make it unwarrantable in him to come and worship Jehovah?

Let us hear how He speaks to the sons of men, Jew and Gentile:-- "Make a joyful noise unto God, all ye lands! Sing forth the honour of His name, Make His praise glorious." (Psa 66:1)

Again He speaks,-- "O sing unto the Lord a new song; Sing unto the Lord, all the earth! Sing unto the Lord, Bless His name! Show forth His salvation from day to day." (Psa 96:1)

Again He speaks,-- "Praise ye the Lord! For it is good to sing praises unto our God; For it is pleasant; Yea, praise is comely." (Psa 147:1)

Nay, He calls on all nature to praise Him. He claims the homage of the inanimate creation. "Let the heavens rejoice, And let the earth be glad; Let the sea roar, and the fulness thereof. Let the field be joyful, and all that is therein; Then shall the trees of the wood rejoice Before the Lord." (Psa 96:11-13)

Thus is God seeking for worshippers here on earth. And what is His gospel but the proclamation of His gracious search for worshippers? He sends out His glad tidings of great joy, that He may draw men to Himself and make them worshippers of His own glorious self.

The shepherd loses one of his flock; and he misses it. The shepherd misses the sheep more than the sheep misses the shepherd. The sheep is too precious to be lost. It must be sought for and found; whatever toil or peril may be in the way. Even life itself is not to be grudged in behalf of the lost one, "The good Shepherd giveth His life for the sheep," as if the life of the sheep were more valuable than that of the Shepherd.

The woman loses one of her ten silver pieces, she cannot afford to lose it. She must have it back again. She seeks till she find it. It does not miss her, but she misses it. She seeks and finds!

The father loses his son; and is troubled. The son may not miss the father, but the father misses the son; nor can he rest till he has taken him in his arms again, and set him down at his table with gladness and feasting.

But the passage we are considering brings before us something beyond all this. It is not the shepherd seeking his sheep, nor the woman her silver, nor the father his son; it is Jehovah seeking worshippers! and He is in earnest. He wants to be worshipped by the sons of Adam. He desires the worship of earth no less than that of heaven. He has the praise of angels, but He must have that of men. Such is the value He sets upon us, and such is His love?

But it is spiritual worship, and spiritual worshippers that He is seeking: "The Father seeketh such to worship Him." The outward man is nothing, it is the inner man He is in quest of. The worship must come, not from the walls of the temple, but from the innermost shrine. It must be something pervading the man's whole being, and coming up from the depths of the soul; otherwise, it is but as sounding brass or a tinkling cymbal. Forms, sounds, gestures, dresses, ornaments, are not worship. They are but

"Mouth-honour breath, Which the poor heart would fain deny, but dare not."

Instead of constituting worship, these outward things are often but excuses for refusing the inward service. Man pleases himself with a sensuous and theatrical externalism, because he hates the spiritual and the true. God says, "Give me thine heart." Man says, "No; but I will give you my voice." God says, "Give me thy soul." Man says, "No; but I will give Thee my knee and my bended body." But it will not do. "God is a spirit, and they that worship Him must worship Him in spirit and in truth."

But what provision has God made for all this? It is not enough to say to us, "Be worshippers,"--this might be said to the unsinning, and they would at once comply. "Let all the angels of God worship Him." But say this to a sinner, and he will ask, "How can I, a man of unclean lips and unclean heart, approach the infinitely holy One? It would not be safe in me to come, nor would it be right in God to allow me to approach." There must be provision for this;-- something which will satisfy the sinner's conscience, remove the sinner's dread, win the sinner's confidence, on the one hand, and satisfy God, vindicate right-eousness, magnify holiness, on the other.

For this there is the twofold provision of the blood and the Spirit. The blood satisfies God's righteousness and the sinner's con-science. The Holy Spirit renews the man, so as to draw out his heart in worship. It is the blood that propitiates, and it is the Spirit that trans-forms. God presents this blood freely to the sinner; God proclaims His desire to give this Spirit freely.

"May I use this blood?" perhaps one says. Use it! Certainly. Thou fool, why shouldst thou ask such a question? Use it! Yes; for thou must either use it, or trample on it. Which of these wilt thou do?

"May I expect the Spirit?" some one may say. Expect Him! What! art thou more willing to have the Spirit than God is to give Him? Art thou so willing, and God so unwilling? Thou fool, who has persuaded thee to believe such a lie?

God has come to thee, O man! saying, "I want thee for a worshipper": wilt thou become one? Remember, thou must either be a worshipper or a blasphemer; which wilt thou be?

[14] These are defended on the ground that they teach certain truths. But worship is not for teaching; it is for the taught. To multiply teaching and symbols is to injure worship; for teaching is not worship, and worship is not teaching.

[15] The name Father occurs but seldom in the Old Testament; and not in the same sense as that in which our Lord here uses it. In such places as Deuteronomy 32:6, Isaiah 63:16, 64:8, Jeremiah 31:9, the word refers specially to Jehovah's relationship to Israel, as head of the family; but in our Lord's words the reference is to the great spiritual Fatherhead inherent in His nature, as the invisible God, Jehovah, the being of beings, God over all, head and parent of the universe: not in the modern sense of an equal fatherhood, into the possession of which every man is born; but in the sense contained in the words "we are His offspring" (Acts 17:28), and "in Him we live, and move, and have our being."

Chapter 10

God Seeking Temples

God began with seeking worshippers, but he goes on to seek temples; or rather, in the sense which we are now to consider, in seeking worshippers he was seeking temples; and in preparing worshippers, he was preparing temples.

The Church is the great temple. Each saint is a temple. In His Church, and in each member of that Church, Jehovah dwells. "Ye are builded together for AN HABITATION OF GOD through the Spirit" (Eph 2:22).

Man was made for God to dwell in. Man thrust God out of His dwelling-place, and left Him homeless; without a habitation on earth. The universe was His; every star was His; every mountain was His: but none of these did He count fit to be His habitation. Only in the human heart would He be satisfied to dwell.

Man thrust out God from His dwelling, but God would not be thus driven away. He must return; and He must return in a way which would make it impossible that He should ever be thrust out again; and He must return in a way such as will show not only the hatefulness of man's sin in thrusting Him out, but the largeness of His own grace, and the perfection of His righteousness.

Jehovah is bent upon returning to His old dwelling-place. He might have created others, and dwelt in them. But He has purposed not to part with His old ones. It is as if He could not afford to lose these, or could not bear the thought of casting them away. "I will return," He says. He casts a wistful eye upon the ruins of His beloved dwelling-place, and He resolves to return and rebuild, and re-inhabit.[16]

When the Son of God was here, He had no place to lay His head. He was a homeless man in the midst of earth's many homes. But still He did come, seeking a home, both for Himself and for the Father. The home that He sought was the human heart; and He came with this message from the Father,-- "I will dwell in them." To this closed heart He comes, in loving earnestness, seeking entrance, that He may find for Himself and for the Father a home. Thus He speaks: "Behold, I stand at the door and knock: if any man hear my voice and open the door, I will come in unto him, and will sup with him, and he with me" (Rev 3:20); and again He speaks, "We will come unto him, and make our abode with him" (John 14:23). So that this is our message to the sons of men,--the Father wants your heart for His dwelling,--the Son wants your heart for His dwelling.

But it is for more than dwelling that God is seeking. It is for a temple. To dwell in us, in any sense, would be infinite honour and blessedness. But to take us for His temples, to make us His Holy of Holies, His shrine of worship, His place of praise, His very heaven of heavens, is something beyond all this. Yet it is temples that God is now seeking among the sons of men; not marble shrines, nor golden altars, with fire, and blood, and incense, and gorgeous adornings; but the spirit of man, the broken and the contrite heart.

The Church is God's temple. "In whom ALL THE BUILDING, fitly framed together, groweth into AN HOLY TEMPLE in the Lord" (Eph 2:21). Each saint is God's temple. "Ye are the temple of God" (1 Cor 3:16). Our body is God's temple. "Know ye not that your body is the temple of the Holy Ghost" (1 Cor 6:19).[17]

God is seeking temples on earth,--living temples, constructed of living stones, founded on the one living stone,-- "built up a spiritual house" (1 Peter 2:5).

Of this temple God is Himself the Architect, and the Holy Spirit is the BUILDER. It is constructed after the pattern of heavenly things, according to the great eternal plan, which the purpose of the God, only wise, had designed for the manifestation of His own glory. As both the Architect and Builder are divine, we may be sure that the plan will be perfect, and that it will be carried out in all its details without failure, and without mistake. It will be beauty, completeness, and perfection throughout,--a glorious Church, without spot or wrinkle, or any such thing; in size, in symmetry, in ornament, in majesty, in stability, altogether faultless,--the mightiest and the fairest of all the works of Jehovah's hands.

In another sense, hereafter, when all things are made new, "the Lord God Almighty and the Lamb" are the temple (Rev 21:22). But we also are the temple; both now and hereafter. Both things are true. He in us, and we in Him. We are God's temple, and He is ours for ever.

The foundation is Christ Himself (1 Cor 3:11; Isa 28:16; 1 Peter 2:4-6). He is the rock on which we are builded; He is no less the foundation-stone which bears up the building, and knits its walls together. In the eternal plan of the divine Architect, this foundation-stone is grandly prominent,--the chief part of God's eternal purpose; framed by God; laid by God in the fulness of time; laid in Zion; laid once for all: a sure foundation, a tried stone; one, without a rival and without a second. It was this stone, laid by God, which the apostle (if we may carry out the figure which he uses in connection with his own ministry) carried about with him from place to place, when he went through the gentile world founding churches. "According to the grace of God which is given unto me, as a wise master-builder, I have laid THE FOUNDATION...For other foundation can no man lay than that is laid, which is Jesus Christ" (1 Cor 3:10,11). On this foundation each soul rests. From the first saint, downward to the last, it has been and it shall be so. There is but one foundation for Old Testament saints as well as for new. On this, too, the Church of God rests; the one Church from the beginning, the one body, the one temple, filled with the one Spirit, for the worship of the one Jehovah. Not two foundations, nor two temples, nor two bodies, nor two Churches; but ONE, only one, made up of the redeemed from among men, bought with the one blood, justified with the one righteousness, saved by the one cross, expectants of the one promise, and heirs of the one glory.

The stones are the saints, (1 Peter 2:5) "Unto whom coming as unto a living stone, ye also as lively (living) stones, are built up a spiritual house." Of the quarrying, the hewing, the polishing, the building, of these living stones I cannot here write. But each has a history of his own. Though dug out of one rock, hewn, polished and fitted in by one Spirit, yet each has come to be what he is by means of a different process, some longer, some shorter, some gentler, some rougher. But on the one foundation, they are all placed by the one hand, one upon the other, in goodly order, according to the one eternal plan in Christ Jesus our Lord; forming the one glorious temple for Jehovah's worship and habitation. Many stones, one temple; many members, one family; many branches, one vine; many crumbs, one loaf. They are "BUILDED TOGETHER for an habitation of God through the Spirit." The "unity of the faith," (Eph 4:13), from the beginning is the pledge of the unity of the temple; and as this faith has been one since the day of the announcement of the woman's seed, so has this temple been; the multitude of stones not marring but enhancing the unity. The "unity of the Spirit," too, (Eph 4:3), is both the pattern and the pledge of the temple's unity. It has been one spirit and one temple from the beginning; not two spirits and two temples, but only one. "There is one body and one spirit, even as ye are called in one hope of your calling; one Lord, one faith, one baptism, one God and Father of all, who is above all, and through all, and in you all." Thus all the "building fitly framed together groweth unto an holy temple in the Lord" (Eph 2:21). God is now seeking these stones for His temple among the lost sons of Adam. Worthless and unfit in themselves for use in any divine building, they are sought out and prepared by the great Builder for their place in the eternal building. Yes, God is in search of these stones now; just as He has been these many ages, since Adam, and Abel, and Seth, and Enoch, and Noah, were sought out nd fitted in to form the glorious line or row of stones lying immediately above the foundation-stone. God is coming up to each son of man, degraded as he may be, an outcast, and saying, "Wilt thou not become a stone in my temple? I seek thee: wilt thou prefer thy degradation, and reject the honour which I present to thee."

The temple is holy (1 Cor 3:17; Psa 93:5). It is set apart for God; it is to be used for sacred purposes; it is pure in all its parts; its vessels, its walls, its gates, its furniture. It is not yet perfect, but it shall one day be so. Into it nothing that defileth shall enter. And even now God, the inhabitant of the temple, is seeking holiness of all who belong to it. "Be ye holy, for I am holy."

Let us dread the defilement of His temple; for it is written, "If any man defile the temple of God, him shall God destroy" (1 Cor 3:17). For God will not be mocked, nor allow His throne to be polluted. Yet do we not defile it by sin, by worldliness, by vanity, by formality, by profanity, by our unfragrant incense, our impure praises and prayers?

Let us rejoice in the honour of being living temples, living stones, consecrated to the service of the living God. Let us walk worthy of the honour,--the honour of being filled with God, penetrated by His light, perfumed by His sweetness, gladdened by His love, and glorified by His majestic presence and indwelling fulness.

[16] "The designation was most apt, of so excellent a creature, to this office and use, to be immediately sacred to Himself and His own converse: His temple and habitation, the mansion and residence of His presence and indwelling glory! There was nothing whereto he was herein designed whereof His nature was not capable. His soul was, after the required manner, receptive of a deity; its powers were competent to their appointed work and employment; it could entertain God by knowledge and contemplation of His glorious excellencies, by rev-

erence and love, by adoration and praise. This was the highest kind of dignity whereto creature nature could be raised,--the most honourable state. How high and quick an advance! This moment nothing; the next, a being capable and full of God."-- Howe's Living Temple.

[17] In all these passages the word used signifies the inner part or shrine of the building,--the holy place and the holy of holies. We are the holy of holies, where the cherubim dwelt, where Jehovah dwelt, where He is said to "dwell between the cherubim"; or as it really is, to "inhabit the cherubim"; the cherubim being His habitation. Into this inner shrine the blood was brought, but not the fire. The effects of the fire were there, the smoking incense, but not the fire itself; for into this sanctuary no wrath can enter. The wrath has been expended and exhausted outside; and this sanctuary is the abode of love and favour; they who belong to it have been delivered from wrath for ever. They are the monuments of exhausted wrath,--wrath which has spent itself upon another, and which has passed away from them for ever. I may notice that it was into the holy place, that Judas threw the pieces of silver,--going to the gate, and flinging them in among the priest as they were carrying on the service.

Chapter 11

God Seeking Priests

If God has a temple, He must have priests; else were there no song, no service, no worship. In His eternal plan, priesthood is provided for; a priesthood not of angels but of redeemed men; of those who seemed the least likely to fulfil such an office in such a temple.

It is a "holy priesthood" that he has provided (1 Peter 2:5). It is a "royal priesthood" (1 Peter 2:9); for He has made us kings and priests. It is a heavenly priesthood like that of His own Son.

As such we minister at God's altar, we tread His courts, we eat His shew-bread, we kindle and trim His lamps, we offer His sacrifices, we burn His holy incense.

God is seeking priests among the sons of men. A human priesthood is one of the essential parts of His eternal plan. To rule creation by man is His design; to carry on the worship of creation by man is no less part of His design.

He is now in search of priests; and He has sent His Son to prepare such for His temple. In order to their being such, He must redeem them; He must reconcile them; He must cleanse them; He must clothe them with the garments of glory and of beauty. All this He does. "The Son of man came to seek and to save that which was lost."

The embassy of peace which is going forth from the cross is an embassy in quest of priests. His ambassadors of peace beseech men to be reconciled to God in order to their becoming priests. God Himself in His glorious gospel comes up to the sinner and asks him to become a priest to Him.

And what does this priesthood mean? What does it embrace? Let us consider this.

Priesthood is the appointed link between heaven and earth; the channel of intercourse between the sinner and God. God and man can only come together on the ground of mediatory priesthood. Such a priesthood, in so far as expiation is concerned, is in the hands of the Son of God alone; in so far as it is to be the medium of communication between Creator and creature, is also in the hands of redeemed men,-- of the Church of God.

Sin had broken up all direct or open intercourse, as we have seen; and the veil declared this. All access to God was to be debarred till a new medium should be provided, such as should secure the ends of righteousness; such as should make it honourable for the Holy One to receive the unrighteous; and such as should make it safe for the un- holy to stand in the presence of the Holy.

Priesthood is the link between the sinner and God, between earth and heaven,--earth, where all is vile; heaven, where all is pure. Without priesthood, God and we are at awful and unremoveable dis- tance from each other. Without priesthood, there can be no transference of guilt, no remission of sin, no reconciliation to God, no restoration either to fellowship or blessing. Priesthood involves and accomplishes all these, because it is through it that the substitution of life for life is effected. It is the conducting medium through whose agency the exchange is brought about between the sinner and the Surety. In nothing less than this does its purpose terminate, and wherein it falls short of this, it is but a pretext or a name. If priesthood be not the living link between God and the sinner, it is nothing.

All this was exhibited in symbolic rite under the former law. It was through priesthood that all intercourse with God was carried on. It was the priest that led the sinner into God's presence, that presented his offering, that transacted the business between him and God, and that received the blessing from God to bestow upon the sinner. God set up the Aaronic priesthood on very purpose to exhibit this; to let men know what His idea of priesthood was, and what He intended a priest to be.

True, this ancient priesthood had only to do with the flesh; it pertained but to the outward person of the sinner, and the mere visible courts of God. It could not reach the inner man; it could not take hold of the conscience; it could not lead the worshipper into the true pres- ence of the invisible Jehovah. It fell short of these ends, and thus far was defective. Still, it did fully accomplish its end as a medium of communication, in so far as the outward man and the material courts were concerned. It was complete according to its nature; and in so far as it went, it established intercourse between the sinner and God.

In so doing, it brought out most fully God's idea of priesthood, as if to prevent the possibility of any mistake upon the point. It showed God's ultimate design in regard to this; His intention of bringing in a perfect priesthood in His own time and way. His object was not to show men how to construct and set up a priesthood of their own, but to tell them what He Himself meant to do, so as to hinder their attempting such a thing. His object was to teach them the true meaning of priesthood, in order that when He brought in His own High Priest, they might fully understand the nature of His work, and the end to be accomplished. It was a new and a great idea that He sought to teach them, an idea which would never have occurred to themselves; an idea which it required long time to unfold to them; an idea most needful for them fully to grasp, as upon it depended the new relationship which grace was to introduce between them and God.

But then when the old priestly ritual had thus served its ends, it was of no more use. It behoved to be taken down, as being more likely to hinder than help forward the sinner's intercourse with God, as being certain to confuse and perplex, and lead to innumerable mistakes in the great question of approach and acceptance. It was not to be imitated, for any imitation would but mislead men from the true priesthood. It was not to be set up in another form, for every part of it was merged, and, as it were, dissolved irrecoverably in the priesthood of the Son of God. The High Priest of good things to come had absorbed it all into Himself, so that any attempt to reconstruct it in any form is undoing what God has done; restoring what He Himself has taken to pieces; committing sacrilege with His holy vessels; nay, profaning with irreverent touch what He has removed out of sight, and forbidden to be handled or used.

So far, then, is the old ritual from being a model or example for us now, that it forbids the attempt to imitate its rites. Its very nature, so purely symbolic and prospective, forbids such an attempt. Its abolition still more strongly prohibits this. For that abolition is God's proclamation that its ends are served, and its time accomplished. But specially its abolition, through fulfilment in the person of Messiah, declares this. Before it was cast away, everything in it that was of value was gathered out of it, and perpetuated in Him. Every truth that it contained was taken from it, and embodied in Him. It did not pass away simply because its time had come, but because the need for it had ceased; it had been superseded by something infinitely more glorious in its nature, and more suitable to the sinner. Who thinks of preserving the sand when the gold that it contained has been extracted? or who misses the beacon-light when the sun has risen?

The coming of the Son of God, the Great High Priest, thus involves the abolition of priesthood in the old sense, for He has taken it wholly upon Himself: it is now centred in Him. All the ends of priesthood are fully met by Him. There is not one thing which we need either as sinners or as worshippers which we have not in Him. So that the question arises, What end can it serve to set up another priesthood apart from His? Has He left anything incomplete which ought to be completed by us? Has He left any of the distance unremoved between us and God? Has He left the work of atonement, and mediation, and intercession, in such a state of imperfection, that we require a new priestly order to perfect it? If not, then is it not strange profanity, as well as perversity in man, to insist upon setting up what is so wholly unnecessary, and what cannot but cast dishonour upon the divine priesthood of Messiah as being imperfect in itself, and as having failed in its ends?

In the present age, then, there are none on earth exercising priestly functions. There is ministry, but not priesthood. The apostles were not priests. They never claimed the office, and never sought to exercise it in the Church. Nor did they enjoin their successors to claim it, nor give them the slightest hint that, as ministers, they were priests. They taught them that priesthood had passed away; that the priestly raiment had been rent in pieces; that there was no longer any temple, or altar, or sacrifice needed upon earth under this dispensation. The epistle to the Hebrews gives the lie to all priestly pretensions, and the epistles to Timothy and Titus show how totally different ministry is from priesthood.

Yet we read of the "royal priesthood" (1 Peter 2:9); we read of "kings and priests"; we read of those who claimed to themselves the priestly name even here. But these were not apostles, nor prophets, nor evangelists, but simply saints. As saints, they were priests. As one with the Great High Priest, they were entitled to this name. As those who were called to share with Him the future honours of the throne and altar, they are the "royal priesthood." Other priests upon earth there are none. Usurpers of the name and office there are many. Of true, God-chosen priests, there are none save these.

Their priesthood is still in abeyance, so far as the actual exercise of it is concerned. They are priest-elect; but, at present, no more. Their title they have received, when brought into the Holy of Holies by the blood of Christ; but on the active functions of priesthood they have not entered. It doth not yet appear what they shall be. They wear no royal crown; they are clothed with no priestly raiments; their garments for "glory and for beauty" are still in reserve among the things that are "reserved in heaven, ready to be revealed in the last time." Both their inheritance and their priesthood are as yet only things of faith; they are not to be entered on till their Lord returns; they are priests in disguise, and no man owns their claim. Yet it is a sure claim; it is a Divine claim; it is a claim which will before long be vindicated. The day of the MANIFESTATION of those priests is not far off. And for this they wait, carefully abstaining from usurping honours and dignities which God has not yet put upon them.

The High Priest whom they own is now within the veil; and till He come forth, they repudiate all priestly pretensions, knowing that at present all sacerdotal office, and authority, and glory, are centred in Him alone. To attempt to exercise these would be to rob Him of His prerogative, to forestall God's purpose, and to defeat the end of the present dispensation.

Their priesthood is after the order of Melchizedek. The King of Salem and priest of the Most High God is he whom they point to as their type. Their great Head is the true Melchizedek; and they, under Him, can claim the office, and name, and dignity. Melchizedek's unknown and mysterious parentage is theirs, for the world knows them not, neither what nor whence they are. Melchizedek's city was Salem; theirs is the New Jerusalem, that cometh down out of heaven from God. His dwelling was in a city without a temple, and He exercised His priesthood without a temple; so their abode is to be in that city of which it is said, "I saw no temple therein, for the Lord God Almighty and the Lamb are the temple of it." Distinct from Abraham, and greater than he, though of the same common family of man, was Melchizedek; so they, "the church of the first-born," distinct from Israel, and greater than they, yet still partakers of a common nature, are to inherit a kingdom more glorious and heavenly than what shall ever belong to the sons of Abraham according to the flesh.

It is in the age to come that they are to exercise their royal priesthood. They are the kings, while the dwellers on earth are the subjects. They are priests, and, as such, carry on the intercourse between earth and heaven.

For priesthood is not merely for reconciliation, but for carrying on intercourse after reconciliation has been effected. It is not merely for securing pardon, but for forming the medium of communication between the pardoner and the pardoned. Thus priesthood may exist after all sin has passed away, and the curse has been taken from sky and earth, and all things have been made new.

For this end shall priesthood exist in the eternal kingdom, both in the person of Christ Himself, and of His saints. A link is needed between the upper and the lower creation; between heaven and earth;

between the visible and the invisible; between the Creator and the created. That link shall be the priesthood of Christ and His redeemed. They shall be the channels of communication between God and His universe. They shall be the leaders of creation's song of praise; from all regions of the mighty universe gathering together the multitudinous praises, and presenting them in their golden censers before Jehovah's throne. Through them worship shall be carried on, and all allegiance presented, and prayer sent up from the unnumbered orbs of space, the far- extending dominions of the King of kings.

Whether the kingly or priestly offices are to be conjoined in each saint, as in Christ Himself, or whether some are to be priests and some kings, we know not. The separation of the offices is quite compatible with the truth as the Church forming the Melchizedek priesthood: for the reference may be to the Church as a body, and not to each individual. And is it not something of this kind that is suggested to us by the four living ones and the four-and-twenty elders in the Revelation? Do not the former look like priests, and do not the latter look like kings?

Yet it matters not. In either way, the dignity is the same to the Church; in either way will the "royal priesthood" exercise their office under Him who is the Great Priest and King.

Our priesthood, then, is an eternal one. There will be room for it, and need for it hereafter, though the evils which just now specially call for its exercise shall then have passed away. We greatly narrow the range of priesthood when we confine it to the times and the places where sin is to be found. Such, no doubt, is its present sphere of exercise; and it is well, indeed, for us that it is so. Did it not extend to this, where should we be? Were it not now ordained specially for the alienated and the guilty, to restore the lost friendship, and refasten the broken link between them and God, what would become of us? But having accomplished this, must it cease? Has it no other region within which it can exercise itself? Has it not a wider range of function, to which, throughout eternity, it will extend, in the carrying out of God's wondrous purposes? And just as the humanity of Christ is the great bond of connection between the Divine and the human, the great basis on which the universe is to be established immovably for ever, and secured against a second fall, so the priesthood of Christ, exercised in that humanity, shall be the great medium of communication, in all praise, and prayer, and service, and worship of every kind; between heaven and earth; between the Creator and the creature; between the King Eternal, Immortal, and Invisible, and the beings whom He has made for His glory, in all places of His dominion, whether in the heaven of heavens, or in the earth below, or throughout the measure-less regions of the starry universe.

Chapter 12

God Seeking Kings

One great part of God's eternal purpose in creation was to rule His universe by a MAN. "Unto the angels hath He not put in subjection the world to come, whereof we speak; but one in a certain place testifieth, What is MAN, that Thou art mindful of him, or the SON OF MAN that Thou visitest him?" (Heb 2:5,6).

To Adam therefore He said, "have dominion," or "rule." After the words of blessing, conveying fruitfulness to man, "be fruitful and multiply," there are three words added, conveying earth over to man as his possession and his kingdom, so that he might exercise authority in it by "divine right." 1. Replenish or fill. 2. Subdue. 3. Rule.

Adam's unfaithfulness, by which dominion was forfeited, did not make the great purpose of none effect. That purpose has stood and shall stand for ever. Instead of the first Adam God brings in the "last Adam," the "second Man," the Lord from heaven, as His King, and He introduces His offspring as kings under Him, to fill, subdue, and rule the earth.

He has found His King, and has put all things under His feet: placing on His head the many crowns, and setting Him on the throne of universal dominion,-- though as yet we see not all things actually put under Him. He says, "Yet have I set my King upon my holy hill of Zion": and He gives Him the heathen for His inheritance and the uttermost ends of the earth for His possession. He is the great Melchizedec,--the priestly King,--into whose hands all things have been put.

But under Him, or associated with Him, are other kings. These are the redeemed from among men,--the chosen according to the good pleasure of His will: by nature, sons of the first Adam, but created anew and made sons of the second.

From the ranks of fallen men God is selecting His kings. He has sent His Son to deliver them from their death and curse. He has sent His Spirit to quicken them and to transform them, not merely into obedient loving subjects, but into kings, heirs of the great throne. "Instead of thy fathers shall be thy children, whom thou mayest make PRINCES in all the earth" (Psa 45:16).

These kings, though by nature mortal men, become heirs of immortality, and at the resurrection of the just, put on all that is to fit them for their everlasting reign. Everything connected with them is of God.

1. God elects them. It is by His will that they are what they are. He finds the race of Adam in the horrible pit, and out of that ruined mass He chooses some,--not only to salvation but to glory and dominion. These kings are the chosen of God.

2. He redeems them. They are found in the low dungeon, captives and prisoners in the hands of the great oppressor. God sends redemption to them,-- redemption through Him who takes their captivity upon Him, that they may be set free; who enters their prison-house, and takes their bonds upon Him that they may be unbound. In Him they have redemption through His blood.

3. He consecrates them. Their consecration is by blood. It is the blood of the covenant that sets them apart for their future work and honour. Sprinkled with the precious blood they are "sanctified" for dominion;--for that holy royalty to which they have been chosen.

4. He anoints them. With that same anointing with which Christ was anointed, they are anointed too,--anointed for royal rule,--priestly-royal rule. The Holy Spirit, dwelling in them, as in their Head, coming down on them, as on their Head, fits them for the exercise of dominion. The wisdom needed for government is a holy wisdom, and this holy wisdom they receive by means of the unction from the Holy One.

5. He crowns them. They are, as yet, only kings- elect. Their coronation-day is yet to come. Yet the crown is already theirs by right; and He who chose them to the throne will before long put the crown upon their head.

Not out of the ranks of angels is He seeking kings. This would not suit His purpose, nor magnify the riches of His grace. Fallen man must furnish Him with the rulers of His universe. Human hands must wield the sceptre, and human heads must wear the crown.

To this honour He is calling us. He is sending out His ambassadors for this end; and the gospel with which they are intrusted is the glad tidings of a kingdom. And this in a double sense. There is a kingdom into which they are to enter and be partakers of its glory: and yet, in the same kingdom, they are to be God's anointed kings. It is a kingdom doubly theirs. They not only "see the kingdom of God" (John

3:3); they not only "enter into the kingdom of God"; but they occupy its thrones. "The kingdom, and the dominion, and the greatness of the kingdom, under the whole heaven, is given to the people of the saints of the Most High, and they possess the kingdom" (Dan 7:22,27). "I appoint unto you a kingdom," says our Lord, "that ye may sit on thrones" (Luke 22:28). "To him that overcometh will I give to sit on my throne, even as I also overcame and am set down with my Father on His throne" (Rev 3:21). Hence they sing the song, "Thou art worthy, for Thou hast redeemed us by thy blood out of every kindred, and tongue, and people, and nation; and hast made us unto our God kings and priests: and we shall reign on the earth" (Rev 5:9). Not to be reigned over, but to reign, is the honour to which they are called. "They shall REIGN for ever and ever" (Rev 22:5).

O sons of men! This is the honour to which God is calling you. It is for the end of making you His kings that He is seeking you. To deliver you from wrath is the beginning of His purpose concerning you; to set you on His throne is the end. Nothing short of this. Think what the riches of His grace must be, and His kindness towards us in Christ Jesus our Lord! Where sin has abounded grace has abounded more. Herein is love! Behold what manner of love the Father has bestowed on us, that we should not only be called sons but kings; that we should not only be lifted to a place in His family, but to a seat upon His throne! To make us in any way or in any sense partakers of His glory and sharers in His dominion is much but to make us "heirs of God and joint-heirs with Christ," is unspeakably more. A throne such as man can give and take away seems to many a worthy object of ambition; how much more the kingdom which God gives, the kingdom which cannot be moved.

And if any one asks, How may I share this royalty and win this crown? we answer in the well- known words, "As many as received Him, to them gave He power (right) to become the sons of God"; for what is true of the sonship is true of the kingship too. We obtain it by receiving the Son of God. He that takes Christ receives a kingdom, and becomes a king. His connection with the King of kings is His security for a throne. Oneness with Christ gives him the royal inheritance. To be washed in His blood, to be clothed with His raiment, to be quickened with His life, to be gladdened with His love, to be crowned with His crown,--these are some of the steps of honour, up which He leads those who believe in His name.

For it is a throne that cannot be bought. It is THE GIFT of "the King eternal, immortal, and invisible"; and He giveth it to whomsoever He will. The invitation which the Son of God gives to us in His gospel is an invitation to a throne and crown. He holds it up and bids us look at it. He holds it out and bids us take it.

I know not if all this were ever better described than by John Bunyan, in the beginning of the "Pilgrim's Progress," in the dialogue between Christian and Pliable:--

"Pli.--Come, neighbour Christian, since there are none but us two here, tell me now further what the things are, and how to be enjoyed, whither we are going.

"Chr.--I can better conceive of them with my mind, than speak of them with my tongue: but yet, since you are desirous to know, I will read of them in my book.

"Pli.--And do you think that the words of your book are certainly true?

"Chr.--Yes, verily; for it was made by Him that cannot lie.

"Pli.--Well said; what things are they?

"Chr.--There is an endless kingdom to be inhabited, and everlasting life to be given us, that we may inhabit the kingdom for ever.

"Pli.--Well said; and what else?

"Chr.--There are crowns of glory to be given us, and garments that will make us shine like the sun in the firmament of heaven.

"Pli.--This is very pleasant; and what else?

"Chr.--There shall be no more crying, nor sorrow: for He that is owner of the place will wipe all tears from our eyes.

"Pli.--And what company shall we have there?

"Chr.--There we shall be with seraphims and cherubims, creatures that will dazzle your eyes to look on them. There also you shall meet with thousands and tens of thousands that have gone before us to that place; none of them are hurtful, but loving and holy; every one walking in the sight of God, and standing in His presence with acceptance for ever. In a word, there we shall see the elders with their golden crowns; there we shall see the holy virgins with their golden harps; there we shall see men that by the world were cut in pieces, burnt in flames, eaten of beasts, drowned in the seas, for the love that they bare to the Lord of the place, all well, and clothed with immortality as with a garment.

"Pli.--The hearing of this is enough to ravish one's heart. But are these things to be enjoyed? How shall we get to be sharers thereof?

"Chr.--THE LORD, THE GOVERNOR OF THE COUNTRY, HATH RECORDED THAT IN THIS BOOK; THE SUBSTANCE OF

WHICH IS, IF WE BE TRULY WILLING TO HAVE IT, HE WILL BESTOW IT UPON US FREELY."

Thus very simply and beautifully does Bunyan put the manner of our obtaining the glory. Some would call this too free. Some would say, Here is the way made far too easy, without any preparatory alarms and repentance. But there stands John Bunyan's idea of the way of a sinner's entrance into the kingdom; and let him who can improve or correct it do so. "The Lord, the Governor of the country, hath recorded that in this book; the substance of which is, If we be truly willing to have it, He will bestow it upon us freely."

Bunyan's soundness of doctrine is well known. His Calvinism was of a very decided kind. His views of Christ's redemption-work were very precise. His belief as to the necessity of the Holy Spirit's work was undoubted; yet he delighted to set forth the gospel in all its scriptural simplicity, unencumbered with preparatory exercises and processes intended to make the sinner "fit for receiving Christ," and fit for having the peace of the gospel dispensed to him; and never did he state that free gospel more freely, that simple gospel more simply, than when, in the manifest fulness of his heart, he wrote the above sentence, and put it into the lips of his pilgrim:-- "IF WE BE TRULY WILLING TO HAVE IT. HE WILL BESTOW IT UPON US FREELY."

Such a sentence shines like a star; yes, like a star to a tempest-tossed sinner in his night of darkness. He asks, How may I be saved? how may I be made a worshipper? how may I become a temple? how may I be taken into the royal priesthood? God's answer is not, works, and pray, and wait, and get convictions, and bring yourself under the stroke of the law; but believe and live; believe in the Lord Jesus Christ, and thou shalt be saved. Likest in its naked simplicity to these divine utterances is that star- like sentence of the Puritan dreamer. It is but another form, in language all his own, of the concluding message of gladness dropped from heaven, as the great book of truth was about to be closed and sealed:-- "WHOSOEVER WILL, LET HIM TAKE THE WATER OF LIFE FREELY."

Too free! Too easy! Too simple! It will only make skin-deep professors! Another gospel! So say some whose idea of the gospel seems to be that of a work to be done by the sinner, not of a work which Christ has already done; whose exhortations to the inquirer are, Wait, pray, seek, wrestle, labour on, and possibly God may drop salvation into our lap; whose theory of a sinner's approach to a Saviour turns all upon the necessity of some long, laborious preliminary seekings, repentances, convictions, terrors, by which he is so humbled and broken, as to be at length in a right frame for Christ to bless him, in a right condition to be trusted with rest of soul;--whose largest grasp of the glorious gospel extends only to this, that it is good news for the qualified, for those who have been ploughed deep enough and long enough by the law.[18]

Well: go to; go to, we say to such. Away and dispute the matter not with us, but with the Master. Ask Him why He "received sinners" at once, without preliminary work, or qualification, or preparation, or delay; why He said to the hardened profligate of Sychar, "Thou wouldst have asked, and He would have given"; to Zaccheus, "Make haste and come down, for today I must abide at thy house"; to the adulteress, "Neither do I condemn thee"; to the thief upon the cross, "Today shalt thou be with me in paradise." Upbraid Him with allowing three thousand of Jerusalem sinners, at one bound, and under one single message, to pass into the kingdom, instead of keeping them "waiting at the pool," or tortured by the law into gloomy fitness for the glad tidings: express your astonishment that He should have set such an example of rearing churches out of heathen idolaters in a single day,--Corinth, Ephesus, Colosse, Thessalonica, Philippi, without waiting for years before calling their members "saints," or permitting them to sit down at the table of the Lord; set up your foolishness against His wisdom, your presumption against His lowliness, your traditions against His commandments, your love of darkness against His joy in light; proclaim your amended gospel, the gospel of Galatia, "Except ye be circumcised, Christ shall profit you nothing"; but what will be the result of those amendments and restrictions on Christ's free gospel? What will all this wood, and hay, and stubble come to in the great day of the Lord? What will be thought of all these barriers which human self-righteousness has reared to check the speed of the flying man-slayer, and keep him from too easy and too swift an entrance into the city of refuge, when "the breath of the Lord, like an overflowing stream" (Isa 30:28), shall sweep these barriers and their builders clean away.

[18] "Satan would keep souls from believing by persuading them that they are not yet qualified and sufficiently fitted for Christ, and that they have not seen themselves absolutely lost, not so much burdened with sin as they should. And, it is to be feared, that Satan makes use of many of God's ministers, as the old prophet mentioned, 1 Kings 13:11, &c,. to keep off, and drive away souls from Christ, under the notion of

preaching peremptory doctrine for Christ, and so seek to fit men for him, as some have preached many months together this doctrine, before they would preach Christ at all; whereas their commission, and the example of Christ and His disciples, was to preach glad tidings first."--Powel, an old Puritan.

You may also enjoy ...

Wandering Between Two Worlds: Essays on Faith and Art
Anita Mathias
Benediction Books, 2007
152 pages
ISBN: 0955373700

Available from www.amazon.com, www.amazon.co.uk
www.wanderingbetweentwoworlds.com

In these wide-ranging lyrical essays, Anita Mathias writes, in lush, lovely prose, of her naughty Catholic childhood in Jamshedpur, India; her large, eccentric family in Mangalore, a sea-coast town converted by the Portuguese in the sixteenth century; her rebellion and atheism as a teenager in her Himalayan boarding school, run by German missionary nuns, St. Mary's Convent, Nainital; and her abrupt religious conversion after which she entered Mother Teresa's convent in Calcutta as a novice. Later rich, elegant essays explore the dualities of her life as a writer, mother, and Christian in the United States-- Domesticity and Art, Writing and Prayer, and the experience of being "an alien and stranger" as an immigrant in America, sensing the need for roots.

About the Author

Anita Mathias was born in India, has a B.A. and M.A. in English from Somerville College, Oxford University and an M.A. in Creative Writing from the Ohio State University. Her essays have been published in The Washington Post, The London Magazine, The Virginia Quarterly Review, Commonweal, Notre Dame Magazine, America, The Christian Century, Religion Online, The Southwest Review, Contemporary Literary Criticism, New Letters, The Journal, and two of HarperSanFrancisco's The Best Spiritual Writing anthologies. Her non-fiction has won fellowships from The National Endowment for the Arts; The Minnesota State Arts Board; The Jerome Foundation, The Vermont Studio Center; The Virginia Centre for the Creative Arts, and the First Prize for the Best General Interest Article from the Catholic Press Association of the United States and Canada. Anita has taught Creative Writing at the College of William and Mary, and now lives and writes in Oxford, England.
Website: www.anitamathias.com/
Blog: wanderingbetweentwoworlds.blogspot.com/

Breinigsville, PA USA
10 April 2011
259541BV00005BA/29/P

9 781849 028264